WORLD'S MOST
DANGEROUS
JOBS

WORLD'S MOST DANGEROUS JOBS

Summersdale Publishers Ltd
46 West Street
Chichester
West Sussex
PO19 1RP
UK

www.summersdale.com

Printed and bound in the Czech Republic

ISBN: 978-1-84953-292-1

Substantial discounts on bulk quantities of Summersdale books are available to corporations, professional associations and other organisations. For details telephone Summersdale Publishers on (+44-1243-771107), fax (+44-1243-786300) or email (nicky@summersdale.com).

WORLD'S MOST DANGEROUS JOBS

PAULA REID

FOREWORD BY **BEAR GRYLLS**

summersdale

Paula Reid is a motivational speaker and coach. She's a bit of a daredevil, having completed 94 things so far on her list of things to do before she dies, including sailing around the world, walking on hot coals, paddling the Mekong and the Thames, and diving with great white sharks. This is her third book.

CONTENTS

FOREWORD

Life is a great adventure, and a great gift – and our job is to go for it, live it fully, with a smile and to follow our dreams. It ain't rocket science! I know Paula believes in living life to the full – it is what has taken her around the globe.

Paula also understands that sometimes dreams require us to dig deep, to go that extra mile, to distinguish ourselves by our courage and actions. It is this 'extra' that makes the ordinary into the extraordinary; and she has found some extraordinary people for this book.

They have each, in their way, battled the odds that nature and even fellow humans throw at them, whether it's bombs, wildfires or the Southern Ocean. These people are special because they give 100 per cent commitment even when it hurts – with their heart, mind, body and soul. They give total commitment to their most dangerous of professions. And life rewards commitment.

These people push to the limits; they live on the edge. And their actions have earned great respect, and in many cases, great gratitude by those on the receiving end of their courage and resilience.

The wildfire fighters, the RNLI lifeboat crews, the avalanche preventers, the international search and rescue... are all heroes and heroines, risking their lives to save ours.

The astronauts, volcanologists and storm chasers… are pioneers and explorers, expanding our physical and intellectual boundaries.

The Superbike champions, F1 drivers and round-the-world sailors… are extreme sports adventurers, pushing the limits of our physical capabilities.

To me, this book is an insightful and fascinating collection of extraordinary stories told by extraordinary people. And that can only ever be compelling.

Enjoy.

BEAR GRYLLS

INTRODUCTION

I'm an ordinary girl from Sussex with an ordinary upbringing, but I've always believed in living life to the full, and in fulfilling this I have sailed 35,000 miles around the world, paddled the Mekong, kayaked the length of the Thames, run a marathon, walked across the UK, trekked the Inca Trail, lived with the headhunters of Borneo and the cannibals of Papua, walked on hot coals, crewed for the RNLI and mountaineered in Scotland and the Alps. I have bungeed, snowboarded, abseiled, dog sledded, zorbed, skydived, swum with great whites, bog snorkelled, flown over the Grand Canyon and kissed a dolphin…

These adventures help me to feel alive and to know that when I am drawing my last breath, it will be with no regrets.

The inspiration for this book came when I found myself 10,800 feet up Mont Blanc roped to a professional assassin – a trained sniper. He ended up divulging secrets to me that he'd never told anyone else. Once I comprehended the extremities of his profession and the intriguing details in his daily work, I was hooked.

I have always been fascinated by extreme living, extreme worlds, adventures and adventurers. I am drawn to people who, like me, push the limits and break the boundaries of convention or bend the rules of tradition by living life to the full. My life intertwines with these worlds and I am very privileged to know people who accomplish incredible feats and have awe-inspiring adventures in their personal and professional lives.

My original concept for a book was about extreme living: how people handle everyday tasks such as eating, sleeping and peeing in extreme circumstances or environments; I interviewed a lighthouse keeper, a prisoner of war, an Antarctic engineer, a beefeater and a Gurkha. I was interested in those who have to live in extreme environments because of their professions and how it affects their lives: what happens when a sniper wants to sneeze, for example? Snipers can't sneeze whilst on a job of course, because the noise would reveal their position.

The sniper I was roped to while mountaineering showed me his bullet wound scar on his non-firing arm, over a glass of wine in Chamonix. After a few more wines, he relaxed enough to tell me all about his job and confessed that he'd never told anyone so much. Killing people isn't the sort of conversation you have with your close friends and family when you get back from a tour of duty and it's certainly not an aspect of your work that your mum asks you about! But he was OK sharing the harsh reality of his job with a mountaineering buddy in a French bistro surrounded by glaciers and the towering peaks of the Alps, a place where death happens regularly. We'd broken through the etiquette of polite conversation by living dangerously together.

He was surprised that he shared his revelations so easily with me, but I think it was due to the heady mix of adrenaline (post-climb) and alcohol. I was transfixed and asked him more and more probing questions. The stories he told were compelling. The details were surprising and fascinating beyond my imagination. I realised that many other people would be captivated by this sort of story, so the book was reborn as World's Most Dangerous Jobs.

My sniper unfortunately was reticent about being interviewed for the book and for his experiences to be perpetually caught in print. This led to a time-consuming and surreal challenge for me – to find a sniper who was willing to go on record! I gradually realised that they live up to their profession and are hard to find and pin down. It's also not something one can easily advertise, though I did send out a few emails with the header: 'I need a sniper'. I kept waiting for the online police to swoop, especially when I started to research types of sniper rifle, IEDs and covert operations for my undercover cop story.

I ended up doing masses of research into snipers and had all sorts of intriguing and sometimes clandestine conversations with people who shall remain nameless, including senior military personnel, ex-snipers and currently serving snipers, the Ministry of Defence, the Royal Marines Association, Chelsea hospital, the Gurkhas, Kensington Palace, the Small Arms School, beefeaters, Canadian and Australian snipers and a sniper on his satellite phone 'somewhere in the Middle East' who taught me how to stop a sneeze! (Push one finger down hard on the cartilage part of the nose.)

Finally, through a contact of a contact who used to be in the Queen's Regiment, I found Dan Mills who wrote *Sniper One,* and I am very grateful to him for actually saying yes to an interview. Dan's story is incredible as you'll see in my sniper chapter.

The book grew from there. I mainly asked my friends and contacts within my inspirational network of people who live life to the full to become contributors. The fact that I have sailed around the world certainly opened a few doors and some interviewees insisted on hearing about that in return for sharing their stories with me.

Everyone has been really cooperative (thank you, Bear Grylls), lovely (James Toseland) and fascinating (bomb disposal chief) to speak with. I will NEVER forget my interview with the astronaut – it was such a privilege. I am now Facebook friends with the amazing Dave – the US 'Hotshot' firefighter – and I'm desperate to go storm chasing with Roger in the US. I had a real laugh with the jockey and Johnny Herbert, chatted over old times with the RNLI coxswain and round-the-world sailor, had tea and cake over *Star Wars* photos with the stuntman and was surprisingly captivated by the poetic nature of my lovely old Icelandic volcanologist!

I have really enjoyed the journey. I have been absolutely delighted and privileged to speak with such incredible people. I am humbled by their attitudes and experiences and they have collectively reaffirmed my belief in living life to the full. Their lives are certainly lived in the danger zone, but they are all the richer for it.

This is a fascinating and voyeuristic book peering cautiously into the world of extreme jobs, for those who like living life on the edge... or who like to live vicariously through other people's extreme experiences.

Each short account is written in the first person and has been kept in the style of the original character. The fact files have been researched through the interviewees and the Internet. The danger facts contain statistics about the potential for death and injuries involved and the extreme facts are interesting details relating to each job.

There has been genuine excitement and huge interest in this book. I really hope you enjoy reading it as much as I did researching it but I also would like to think that this book will push you to do at least one thing on your bucket list. If the will is there, then there is a way.

You only live once. No regrets.

PAULA REID
Live Life to the Full

THE ASTRONAUT

Extreme rating: ☠☠☠☠☠
Danger level: ▁▄▄▄▅▆▇██
Criteria: Entry is extremely competitive; must be established as a test pilot, engineer, scientist or medic; excellent physical condition
Skills: Team player; good leader; good follower; controlled ego; stamina and ability to deal with stress
Salary: US $64,724–$141,715 (£40,500–£89,000)

Dr Piers Sellers (PhD) OBE is a meteorologist and a NASA astronaut. He is a veteran of three space shuttle missions:

Space Shuttle Atlantis *(7–18 October 2002), a mission to install a truss to the International Space Station (ISS). To do this, Sellers completed three spacewalks and logged 19 hours and 41 minutes of EVA (extra-vehicular activity – work done by an astronaut outside of a spacecraft. It usually refers to a spacewalk but also applies to a moonwalk). The mission was accomplished in 170 orbits, travelling 4.5 million miles in nearly 11 days.*

Space Shuttle Discovery *(4–17 July 2006), a test mission and assembly flight to the ISS. The crew tested new equipment and procedures to increase the safety of space shuttles following the* Columbia *disaster in 2003. They also carried out maintenance on the space station and transferred across supplies, equipment and a new crew member. The mission was accomplished in 306 hours.*

Space Shuttle Atlantis *(14–26 May 2010), the thirty-fourth shuttle to the ISS. On this, Piers was Mission Specialist 4 and lead robotics officer.*

Shuttle crews are usually six or seven people. The pilot and co-pilot are always US citizens and ex-military. The other crew can be from other space agencies or friendly countries. So Canadians, Europeans, Japanese, Russians.

You'd think that it would be difficult working in a small, tight space with different cultures, but actually it works out OK because everyone's from a scientific, technical or flying culture, or sometimes two or three of these. So we have a lot in common; we have similar educations and interests; we are engineers or pilots or scientists. We tend to get along, but there's no time for socialising: everyone's either working hard or so tired you just go to sleep.

Boy, we work hard. Welcome to the 16-hour day. Back to back. Shuttle missions are pretty tiring, they really are. You're trying to get an awful lot done in a short time: maximum value for money and a full agenda.

It's not so much physically tiring because you're in space; you're floating around; you're not really exerting yourself much. That's actually a problem. For the ISS – International Space Station – crews, they have to exercise two hours a day on all these torture machines we have… treadmills, weight machine simulators and stuff like that. It's mentally tiring more than physically because you're trying to keep track of so many things and stay on the timeline and get things done quickly. There are many moving parts to any space mission.

When you get back home you feel exhausted. Mainly physically, because you've been floating around for two weeks and when you come back to earth, gravity just drags you down to the ground – you feel like a little old man. But that goes away after two or three days, then you feel fine again.

We drink water or any other drink that doesn't have alcohol in it. Food is mostly military-like rations: MREs (Meal Ready Eats). But when you get up there, there is a change in the fluid in your body, a lot of it moves north into your head and your taste buds and sense of smell don't work nearly as well in space. So it's like eating cardboard – you eat for effect. I always find it an effort to eat. I have to make it a job. Physically, you lose quite a bit of calcium in orbit and the countermeasure is a lot of exercise which seems to partially offset it.

Spacewalking is the best thing I ever get to do. That's fun, just floating around outside the space station looking down at the earth – just beautiful. It's not like looking through a window into the aquarium, you are *in* the aquarium. You're floating around out there. That's magnificent.

On my first spacewalk, I was the first guy out of the hatch. So we kinda dived out there and I found it completely disorienting for the first few seconds.

Bright, bright light from the sun and a sense of everything moving so fast underneath me and then this gigantic spaceship hanging above me in the black sky. It was magical.

It took me about 30 seconds to get my brain unscrambled. It was really something. Then it did unscramble and I got down to work. All the training kicked in.

You know, it's a very alien environment. You're floating above a planet and you're in free fall. You're bowling along and there's a white sun and a black sky and everything is moving pretty fast. It's extremely beautiful.

The world is very quietly but rapidly turning underneath your feet, 200 miles down and it's quite the sight. You recognise places – it's like looking at maps, but very detailed, very pretty ones. You can see the world moving underneath you. You go around the whole world in 92 minutes. You are doing 5 miles a second travelling at 17,500 miles per hour.

Five miles a second. You go from Land's End to Kent in one minute. I went to school in Kent. I couldn't see the house but I could see Kent very clearly; all the little bumps where Dover and Dungeness are… all those places. You can see the shape of the coastline very clearly.

It never gets tiring to look out the window. Absolutely beautiful.

It never leaves you. Not so much when I'm up there but when I come back, I always have strange dreams. Dreams about floating, about sharp darkness, followed by brilliant light and back again, that kind of thing. It's extraordinary.

I've never felt nervous. The training's very good and it prepares you, at least psychologically, for anything that's coming at you. So, no, I never felt frightened. But all astronauts are frightened of screwing up, how about that? Because of the pressure and the money involved, but they're not frightened of the actual physical danger. You're very well trained for it. It's kind of – 'numbing' is the wrong word, but you get psychologically accustomed to what's coming. People have been doing aviation training for 70 years. And it works. It really works.

But the danger is very real. We built five shuttles, we lost two: one on launch and one on entry (*Challenger* and *Columbia*). So those are probably the most dangerous periods. Spacewalking is dangerous too, but not as dangerous as launch and entry, I think. Don't let anybody tell you this stuff isn't dangerous. It is. When they start selling tickets for people to go up and into orbit, don't be looking for a cast-iron guarantee that it's going to be A-OK at all times. It's not. It's the nature of the beast.

THE ASTRONAUT

I guess I've pushed my chances, numbers-wise. Oh, gosh, I guess I could work it out. If we've lost two crews in 135 missions and I did three. You could do the math… one in twenty-something, I guess. There but for the grace of God, as they say. Everyone's a volunteer in this business, no question about it. Nobody left after *Columbia*. When we lost *Columbia*, pretty much the whole astronaut office stayed in place. Everyone stuck around and worked hard to get things fixed.

There's a lot of discipline and training and military efficiency to the operation, but then it's such a massive undertaking, you never know if something could go wrong. It's too complicated for there not to be a risk of that, and the margins for error are small and the energies are very high. So it's on the edge all the time. You strive for perfect safety, but you know you can't achieve it. But if you don't try, it will definitely be unsafe.

I think the whole business of space exploration will be a pioneering business for some time to come. It's not routine. It really isn't. It is still dangerous and I don't see that changing anytime very soon. I think that's the way it is. Civil aviation now is pretty safe, in fact it's very safe, but early aviation wasn't. When the crossover actually happened, probably sometime in the 1950s or 1960s, it sort of swapped over. So I think we're still back in the barnstorming phase; we're in a sort of 1920s or 1930s equivalent in space flight.

I'm an old aviator [laughs].

STORY TOLD BY PIERS

DANGER FACT:

There have been 18 space flight deaths, including 14 space shuttle astronauts and four Russian Soyuz cosmonauts. There have also been 11 deaths of astronauts and cosmonauts during training.

On 28 January 1986 *Challenger* disintegrated 73 seconds after launch, killing all seven astronauts on board. On 1 February 2003 Columbia disintegrated during re-entry, killing its crew of seven.

EXTREME FACT:

The International Space Station orbits at 205–255 miles altitude. It completes 15.7 orbits per day travelling at a speed of 17,500 miles per hour (approx. 5 miles per second) so the space station sees a sunrise once every 92 minutes!

(NASA, 15 December 2008, 'Current ISS Tracking Data')

THE AVALANCHE
CONTROLLER

Extreme rating: ☠☠☠☠☠
Danger level: ▃▃▄▄■■□□□□
Criteria: Expert skier (not snowboarder); experience in avalanche control or ski patrolling; able to read snowpack and interpret weather conditions; able to observe and correct potential snow hazards; physical fitness; ideally, experience with explosives
Skills: Good work ethic – able to work outside in adverse weather conditions; good people skills; self-motivation
Salary: US $50,000–$60,000 (£31,000–£38,000)

I forecast and control avalanches around our highways in Washington State. My primary focus is the Snoqualmie Pass, which is a busy interstate highway going through a very snowy part of our mountains from Seattle to Boston. We have lots of traffic on that road with heavy snowfalls and avalanche conditions. We average 38 feet of snowfall there each winter – which is quite a bit. It's a big challenge just to keep the roads and driving surfaces in good shape, let alone the hazards the avalanches bring.

Then, in the springtime, I have a different highway that I work on. It's a little two-lane highway, known locally as the Chinook Pass. This area has much more rugged terrain and it's very scenic with a lot of snowfall. We probably see 58 feet here a year. The highway itself is located right in the middle of nearly 100 avalanche paths that affect the road, so it would be impossible to keep it open for any viable period throughout the winter.

We just let it snow in and around mid April, my avalanche crew arrive and we begin avalanche assessments while our maintenance crew clear the snow from the road. Our job there is twofold. First of all it's to keep the maintenance crew safe while they're performing their work, but then our ultimate goal is to eliminate the avalanche risk so that by the time the highway opens (typically end of May or early June), there is very little or no avalanche hazard. We can then leave the area and people can come up and enjoy the recreation – sightseeing, hiking and skiing. In a nutshell, that's what our operations entail.

We look at the snowpack every day and watch the weather. Snowpacks are divided into two primary climates: maritime and continental. The maritime climate, which is where I work, is characterised by very deep snowpack in fairly mild temperatures. So we get lots and lots of snow. It's also not uncommon for us to have rain in the winter. The avalanche conditions that we deal with are very much driven by the weather. So that's a big component of our job: looking at the weather and at the snowpack. Each day we go out, dig into the snow and look at the structure; the different layers and how they're interacting with one another. What we're primarily looking for are weaknesses within the snowpack, weak layers that might be a place where an avalanche would slide. From there, we're looking at what the weather's going to do. Will we receive additional snowfall, or will it turn to rain? Rain or additional snow load can be triggers. As the winter moves toward the spring the sun begins warming the snow, so we need to keep a close eye on those weather conditions. From there, if we determine an area needs our attention, we'll set up avalanche control and blast the slope with explosives.

THE AVALANCHE CONTROLLER

I have a crew of five employees and I look for people who have experience doing avalanche control or ski patrols. They need to have expert skiing ability, a good work ethic, the ability to be outside in very adverse conditions for long periods of time and experience with explosives. A part of our job on the Chinook Pass is triggering avalanches with our skis – what we call 'ski cutting', where we ski across the top of the slope and set off an avalanche. So I need people that are safety-minded in order to do that kind of dangerous task.

We work with explosives and artillery as well. There is definitely a degree of danger to that, but we all enjoy it and want to come back the next day. It looks dangerous, but safety is important, it's a big part of what we do. When you go out and trigger an avalanche with your skis, you've got to do it right or the consequences can be severe. You really need to be in the right place, because if you get caught in an avalanche you only have seconds to get out. Otherwise you're going to be swept down the slope, potentially hitting trees or rocks and get buried. None of that is desirable.

I was caught in one just briefly and was able to get hold of a tree almost immediately, keeping myself from going down the slope. Fortunately, it was right at the start of the avalanche, so as soon as I got hold of the tree, the snow above pushed against me and then within a couple of seconds, it had gone. Then it was just a matter of getting the snow off of my body so I could stand up again. I was lucky that I was near where the avalanche triggered and able to act quickly to get out.

We use different methods with explosives. We throw hand charges, which are like sticks of dynamite, 3 inches diameter by 8 inches long. We ignite a fuse that burns for 90 seconds before it explodes. So that's one method; hand charges thrown on the slope.

Then we use aerial trams which can be as simple as a piece of cable running from one point, say a tree, to another. The explosives are hung from the cable and belayed into the avalanche zone. The hand charges are typically about 2 pounds. The tram shots are anywhere from 25–55 pounds – creating a much, much bigger blast. They're designed to explode in the air above the snowpack and have a much wider range, so they blast the snowpack, shake cliffs or trees and bring down as much snow as possible. They are detonated remotely. We either put a three-minute fuse ignition system into the bag of explosives and send it out on the tram, or we connect that explosive back to our safe area using detonating cord and then ignite it.

Some trams have the cable running at a slightly downhill angle so that the explosives can be belayed out. However, in other cases, we need to deliver explosives across a flat expanse, or even uphill. We have two trams that run alongside the highway and they're powered by stationary bicycles. We climb up a tower, get on a little bicycle, hang the explosive on the cable and pedal! That rotates the cable and sends the explosive up the hill. It's kind of unique. It's a modified unicycle and it's been there for over twenty years.

Europe is probably more technologically advanced than us with push-button control, but we still get there and probably have more fun!

The other thing we have is some surplus military artillery. For areas that we can't access directly, either with a tram or a hand charge, we use the artillery. We have a 105-millimetre recoilless rifle, which is a 1950s vintage. This weapon is due to retire quite soon but it's been our main artillery piece for years. It delivers a 5.5-pound explosive to where we want to trigger an avalanche. More recently, we've augmented that with another piece of artillery – an M60A3 battle tank; a track tank from the 1970s. It's parked on a ridge – we don't drive it around – it just sits there. It also has a 105-millimetre gun, delivering a slightly larger payload of 7 pounds. We climb inside, the turret spins around, we position on our targets, load the weapon and fire. It does a really good job. I never imagined I would fire a tank in my career, but here I am.

We use explosives at Chinook Pass as well, but in a different manner. We go out on the slope where the avalanches start and bury explosives in the snow. This is in the springtime; the snow tends to be more stable in the morning when it's cool, then it becomes unstable during the day as the sun warms the air, heats the snow and puts energy into the snowpack. So we go out in the morning, bury the explosives and we'll put in big shots, like 300–400 pounds, spread out across the slope. That's all connected together with a detonating cord; we'll run that back to the top of the ridge, wait for the conditions to warm and for the avalanche hazard to increase. Then we'll detonate it and get some pretty good results.

It gets quite picturesque and beautiful when those go off.

We need more than a loud noise to trigger an avalanche. It often takes a big shock, and that's where the explosives come into play. The explosives or the weight of a skier moving across the slope will trigger one. Even in our climate, the rain can do it or in new snow, when the conditions are really sensitive, something as small as a snowball landing on the slope can be enough to start an avalanche. That's why we use the trams to shake loose snow down so we don't leave those little triggers out there and have avalanches later on.

A really hard day is one where it's snowing relentlessly for ten, twenty, thirty hours straight. We're doing our best to keep the highway open and there's a lot of traffic, so that complicates it. You almost feel like you're running around chasing your tail; trying to get as much of the snow down and needing to be in a couple places at once. You want everything to be safe but you also want to be able to keep the road going. So that's a big challenge.

Sometimes we'll get an unstable layer of snowpack that will be deeply buried. We call it 'deep slab instability' or a 'persistent weak layer'. The challenge with those is they aren't readily triggered, even with explosives. We had an instance like that a few years ago where we shot a slope repeatedly with the artillery. We got minor amounts of avalanches and felt that we did the work that was appropriate for the area, but about ten, twelve hours later, the slope released – real deep, like 3–5 feet deep, and buried the highway in snow. Fortunately no vehicles were involved. But that's nerve-wracking. To have one get by you like that is wearing. Something like that is difficult to deal with because it's anomalous. At the same time you've got people on the road, they're just driving from one place to another; not concerned with avalanche conditions. But that's my job. You want everybody to be safe.

We're behind the scenes; there's not a lot of visibility with this job. People travelling down the highway don't realise that there is an avalanche team and in many places, our avalanche paths aren't easily visible from the road, they may be obscured by forest or just look like an open slope. A lot of people don't recognise avalanche conditions.

We always carry a pack with rescue gear, radios, extra clothes, food and water. We have collapsible avalanche probes; in case somebody is buried so we can recover them. Around here we equip ourselves so that we could stay out for 12 to 24 hours. At Chinook Pass, we're in a much more remote area, so we carry more gear, additional shelter, a bivvy sack, maybe a small stove – the kind of things that if conditions were bad or if an accident happened, we could stay out for 24 to 48 hours.

We do have amazing scenery; beautiful mountains, big, jagged rocks… The Chinook Pass is right on the edge of Mount Rainier National Park, which is our tallest peak in Washington State at 14,411 feet. It's a very large, impressive volcano. We're in an area that goes from forest to alpine, so you get a lot of variety. There's always new snow and it's really pretty. Occasionally we'll see snowshoe hares, bobcats or foxes and pine martens – they're fairly prolific in the winter. As we move into spring we'll get some eagles and deer and elk migrating from the lowlands back up to their summer grounds in the mountains.

It's something I love to do. There are always unique challenges being thrown at you, whether it's from the snowpack or the weather. I like being out in the mountains and love being in the snow. We hike, we ski uphill, we ski tour quite a bit.

I've done ski cutting in some very active avalanche conditions, getting really big avalanches to trigger from our skis while a thunderstorm moves in. There's darkness, lightning and thunder, avalanches coming down… very north-west, volcanic scenery. It's the kind of situation that keeps me coming back day after day.

STORY TOLD BY JOHN

In February 1910, Wellington, Washington there was a blizzard for nine days. On the worst day, 11 feet of snow fell followed by rain and a warm wind. Just after 1 a.m. on 1 March, there was a lightning strike and a 10-foot-high mass of snow, half a mile long and a quarter of a mile wide, fell towards the town, killing 96 people.

In 1993, an avalanche in Turkey killed 60 people. In France in 1999, 10,594,400 cubic feet of snow slid down a slope, reaching a maximum speed of 60 miles per hour, killing 12 people in their chalets trapped under 16 feet of snow. Also in 1999, an avalanche flowed into an Austrian village at 186 miles per hour, killing 31. In France in one winter season on average 31 people die due to avalanches.

Research carried out in Switzerland based on 422 buried skiers estimates that chances of survival drop very rapidly from 92 per cent within 15 minutes to 30 per cent after 35 minutes to approximately 0 per cent after two hours.

THE BOMB DISPOSAL
EXPERT

Extreme rating: ☠☠☠☠☠
Danger level: ▁▁▃▄▅▆▇█
Criteria: Soldier or officer training; a technical or scientific bias; ammunition technical and explosive engineering training; bomb disposal training
Skills: Numeracy and literacy; dexterity; spatial awareness; good communication skills; calm under pressure; emotionally stable; ability to manage risk
Salary: £35,000 (US $54,000) basic as a captain on entry

I served in the British Army for 27 years and spent most of my time as an ammunition technical officer (ATO) or bomb disposal expert, responsible for explosive safety, ammunition matters and bomb disposal. In my final appointment in the army I was the principal ammunition technical officer, the army's officer responsible for explosives safety and counter terrorist bomb disposal.

I joined the army and the Royal Army Ordnance Corps (now part of the Royal Logistic Corps) with the sole intention of becoming an ammunition technical officer. I knew from an early age that I wanted to specialise in bomb disposal. As a young captain I attended the

27

15-month ammunition technical officers' course which trained us on electronics, nuclear physics, thermodynamics, chemistry, the science of explosives, ballistics; basically, all you need to know to underpin a technical profession based on explosive safety. The first half of the course at the Royal Military College of Science was predominantly theory based; the second half, at the Army School of Ammunition in Warwickshire, was very much about practical experience. Hands-on bomb disposal, and that's when you really find out whether you are cut out for it.

I spent most of my career involved in counter-terrorism and what the Americans now call 'counter-IED' – countering the insurgent and terrorist use of the improvised explosive device. It's a specialist role, not what many people would describe as a mainstream career.

The IED is not a new phenomenon. The first major, high-profile IED attack was probably back in the days of Guy Fawkes' attempt to blow up the Houses of Parliament. The British Army has faced numerous IED campaigns since World War Two. It's a very simple and effective form of attack, being used by many terrorist and insurgent groups. It really came to the fore in the 1960s in Hong Kong and Cyprus and the Northern Ireland campaign in the early 1970s. The high-profile IED campaigns came about in Afghanistan and Iraq; it was in Iraq in late 2004/early 2005 when we started to see many coalition casualties incurred as a result of the terrorist and insurgent use of IEDs; most of the casualties the British Army sustained in recent campaigns have been caused by them.

I think all war's dirty but the IED is a very effective form of attack; it's what the army calls 'asymmetric warfare'. It's a means by which a significantly weaker adversary can attack a more technically capable, stronger enemy. For all our technological superiority in terms of weapons, stand-off attack, detection systems, a small, cheaply buried IED in Afghanistan neutralises many of those technological advantages that the British and the United States have as First-World armies. So in some respects, it's viewed as the weapon of the weak against the strong. It's a very easy way of levelling the odds.

It seems to be relatively easy to make IEDs; many people now have access to knowledge and information about bomb-making. Certainly for the lone-wolf jihadist sitting in his bedroom, agonising over what society's done to him… It's much easier for that person now to go online and come up with recipes for the mixing of explosives, construction details and how to fabricate improvised explosive devices. That's what the internet has done for us. That's not to say all of the mixtures on the internet are safe and easy to produce; they're not at all. Some of them are extremely hazardous, and we see time and time again people blowing themselves up as a result of incautiously following recipes they have downloaded off the internet.

I guarantee that if I went into your garden shed or kitchen, I could come up with the makings of a reasonable-sized improvised explosive device. Terrorist groups now use things like fertilisers, powders used in the fabrication of paints… common, everyday substances used to make very effective explosives.

The management of risk is really critical. One of the problems we've got is that if you subject people to very high levels of activity and very high levels of risk, over long periods of time, they change their perception of what is normal. If you put them into incredibly hazardous, dangerous situations, they will treat that as the norm. People under immense psychological stress will start to take shortcuts. We're training that out of people, but we've got to accept that you can only push people so far. There comes a time when, inevitably, they will recalibrate their own personal risk meters. It's the job of the command structure to recognise that and to pull people out in time. But it gets very difficult. On certain occasions, we've been under immense pressure and taken casualties.

We've sometimes had only a few operators trained to the right level, and that puts immense stress and strain on those people who are in the field at the time. Checks and balances are in place to try to ensure that people aren't taking unnecessary risk, but frequently it's a very difficult call.

Certainly most of the operators I know find themselves in a position where they don't want to let the side down. They recognise that they're in a very difficult position; they don't want to cut corners, nor do they want to walk away from the job. If they don't do it, who will?

There have been times in the recent past where we've just simply not had enough teams or operators on the ground to do the large number of jobs they've been called upon to deal with. In 2008, we saw about a 120 per cent increase in the use of IEDs in Afghanistan; in 2009, about 400 per cent; and in 2010, about 250 per cent. So we've seen an exponential increase in IED activity without the same increase in teams on the ground, because it takes a long time to train these teams, and time to properly equip them.

I know operators who have worked extremely hard over many months because of the needs of the job. Certainly in late 2008 through to late 2010, a lot of the operators were working incredibly hard in Afghanistan. It was not unusual at that time for them to be dealing with over 100 devices in a six-month tour. You contrast that with many operators that served in Northern Ireland. In a similar six-month tour, they would be doing probably one quarter or a third of the number of jobs. But also in Northern Ireland, the conditions were far less environmentally arduous: the temperature, the dust, the sand… it's very debilitating.

The British model for high-threat bomb disposal operations is a core team of four people. So you've got the operator – the high-threat IED disposal operator who's the team leader, and it's he or she who is responsible for going forward alone and exposing themselves to risk. There is then the team number two, the second in command, who is also an ammunition technician and in years to come will become an operator. So it's on-the-ground training for them.

There is also an electronic countermeasures operator, a member of the Royal Corps of Signals, and they deal with the electronic warfare aspects of the job. There's a hugely significant, classified battle going on at all times between bomb makers and those responsible for the building and delivery of electronic countermeasures. I can't go into any more detail than that. But defeating radio-controlled bombs requires very sophisticated countermeasure systems and there's a member of the team responsible for specifically running those. Very much the unsung hero of the team because without them we'd take many, many more casualties. Many of these ECM operators have been wounded in action.

The final member of the team is the escort; the bodyguard. That person is responsible for looking after the operator and the team. The operator will be very much focused on doing the job in hand, and so you want someone who's in a position where they can look outwards, interface and talk with the infantry on the ground, and make certain that the team and the operator are safe.

Probably the best technical countermeasure example would be when the Provisional IRA had some very, very competent bomb makers. In fact, one of the guys they had doing their research and development on radio control devices was a guy called Richard Clark Johnson. He was an American scientist that worked on some US NASA projects. He had some very significant security clearances from the US and he developed a whole range of very, very sophisticated radio command initiation systems. And those radio control systems required the British forces to develop – very, very quickly – suitable countermeasures. The enemy will do one thing, we'll do another… so it's measure, countermeasure, counter-countermeasure, counter-counter-countermeasure; it's a constant battle and one that we need to win if we are going to keep our people alive.

We saw a very similar battle going on in Iraq. Most of the really significant technology came from Iran and the Iranian government were funding a lot of the very advanced developments in IED technology. So most of the British soldiers that were killed in Basra and a high percentage of the Americans that were killed in Baghdad were killed as a result of the Iranian technology that was introduced into that theatre. One of the things that the army needs to do of course is develop 'weapons intelligence' procedures to recognise where new technology is coming from and what we can do to identify the bomb makers; there's a whole range of activities that go on in that sphere to stay one step ahead.

I enjoyed working with the Americans in Baghdad. It was an extraordinarily exciting time and the insurgents and terrorists had really cottoned on to the IED as an effective form of attack. It was good working with an army that wasn't resource constrained – if you wanted something you simply had to ask for it. My work took me onto the streets of Baghdad and I saw first-hand some horrific suicide IED attacks that had targeted civilians. A friend of mine, Pete, was also critically injured whilst working with a US weapons intelligence unit. As I walked around the area where Pete had been blown up, and we found a further victim-operated device, the hazards associated with this occupation really struck me. I started to question the whole assumption that it could never happen to me. If an operator as good as Pete could be injured, then anyone could be injured or killed.

The 'bomb suit' is designed to give you a certain level of protection as you're walking to the device and walking away from it. It gives you minimal protection once you're over the device because it just would not be possible to produce something that could give you good protection with a significant quantity of explosive. It's quite heavy; quite cumbersome; it interferes with your spatial awareness because it makes your body feel like the Michelin man; it makes you less dexterous because you have limited movement in your joints; it certainly slows you down (you can't move very quickly in a bomb suit); and it's also very difficult to use in extreme heat. You get hot very, very quickly. That's one of the reasons why you don't see many operators wearing bomb suits in Afghanistan. It's so difficult environmentally for the operator to wear.

I've worn the bomb suit in the past. It's good for certain jobs. If you're dealing with postal devices that tend to have very small quantities of explosive it can give you good protection. Utterly useless, though, for large devices. And in situations where you're dealing with victim-operated devices, booby traps… positively hazardous, because your lack of spatial awareness puts you at more risk. There is a time and a place for the bomb suit, and the army mandates it in certain situations, but my view is: let the operator decide whether he really wants it on a particular task.

The British Army invented the bomb disposal robots. In good old British Army fashion, we call ours 'Wheelbarrows', so we went from the Mark 1 Wheelbarrow in 1972 through to the Mark 8 which is currently in service. These are absolutely vital. The use of robotics systems – I've got no doubt at all – has saved many bomb disposal operator lives. You could say not being there is always the best countermeasure and bomb disposal conducted at 328 feet is invariably more forgiving than bomb disposal at 6 inches. What the robotics systems do is allow the operator to determine what the device is from a safe distance and also to fire a disruptor or a weapon to disable it before he or she goes forward to make it safe. So I'm a real fan of bomb disposal robots. I've destroyed three of them in my career! They're very expensive, but while you can replace equipment, you can't replace people. I've got no doubt at all that robotics systems are definitely the way to go, but there is only so much you can do with a robot. There's only so much you can do looking at the target through a colour TV camera. In every bomb disposal incident, the operator invariably has got to go forward alone and deal with what he or she finds there. You can't do everything remotely.

The bomb disposal robot used in the film *The Hurt Locker* is an American system produced by QinetiQ Foster-Miller called TALON. There's a whole variety of bomb disposal systems out there. The ones developed by the UK tend to be slightly bigger but they're very robust and are designed to do a whole range of tasks. Some of the smaller robots are good at doing one particular task well. When we're called upon to deal with car bombs, for example, you need a bigger remote control vehicle.

Some of the latest bomb disposal robots have a dozen cameras on them, so you've got superb optical systems, manipulation systems and a whole variety of weapons that you can use. The technology is going forward in leaps and bounds; but we're getting to the stage now where I think the technology is a long way in front of the appetite. Most operators have got a view about what they want to do with a remote control system and that doesn't necessarily mean they need to do every single thing with it.

Also, you've got to bear in mind the cost and expense of very sophisticated robot systems. The latest generation of the British system is nearly £1 million (US $1.6 million) a shot. You'd say: what price is life? And I'd agree entirely that given the choice between destroying an expensive robot and having someone risk their life, I would go with the robot every single day of the week. In bomb disposal, life is paramount, time and property are secondary considerations.

There's a whole sophisticated array of search and detection equipment, which I can't go into. The operator will always work in high-threat situations with a Royal Engineer search team. That team is equipped, configured and trained specifically to seek out and search for IEDs. It's an incredibly difficult and dangerous job that those guys do. I certainly wouldn't want to get on the ground without a Royal Engineer search team and they've sustained very high numbers of casualties: people killed and seriously injured looking for low-metal content devices with detection systems that are good but not perfect. And of course, the British Army relies very heavily on dogs. We've spent millions of pounds trying to detect using electronic and chemical systems but none of these are as good as a dog's nose. The long and the short of it is, to detect buried IEDs you need a range of systems, a range of capabilities and some very brave people to operate them. The high-threat operator may be at higher risk when he or she is dealing with a device; a member of a Royal Engineer search team faces a significant degree of risk from the moment they leave a forward operating base until the moment they return. I wouldn't want to do their job.

There are generic categories of IED. The basic ones are: time-initiated; victim-operated (like booby traps which the victim initiates); command initiation and suicide initiation. Most of the devices that are being encountered in Afghanistan at the moment are either command-initiated or overwhelmingly victim-operated. These use simple, improvised pressure plates that are buried in the ground, wired up to a battery and explosives, and are incredibly effective. So from the surface, you see nothing – very simple technology, very, very cheap to make. The home-made explosive is based on locally available fertiliser and the chemical that it's mixed with. They're incredibly easy to fabricate.

It varies from province to province in Afghanistan. You're probably looking at about 75 per cent of devices being victim-operated, so the pressure plate variety. About 20 per cent are command-initiated. This is either radio controlled or what we call 'command wire', where there's a physical wire that connects the firer of the IED to the device itself and they close a simple switch when the target presents itself. The final category can include suicide missions. We see very few of those, but they tend to be very effective. An American colonel I worked for in

Baghdad referred to the suicide IED as the terrorist's precision guided munition – the terrorist's cruise missile. There are not many of them, but they use them against high-value targets and targets that are very difficult to attack in other ways.

It's not just about neutralising the bomb. From the moment the operator arrives, he wants to understand, why is the bomb there? What was the terrorist or insurgent trying to achieve by putting the bomb there? It's not just a question of dealing with what he's got. Even before he starts working on the device, the first thing he'll do is ask: is the local population safe? Are the troops safe? Is his team safe? Is he safe? And he'll do it in that order. So it's about determining that they've got a safe place in which to operate. They may well need to increase the danger area in order to deal with the device. The operator will want to determine: what has happened? What's been seen? Can he talk to the witnesses? Has anyone been up to the device? If they have, can he speak to them? What was heard? Is there anything unusual going on in the area? And having assimilated all of this information, he'll formulate his render safe procedure (RSP). And that render safe procedure will be dynamically altered based on information that comes in.

He will try to do things remotely; using his robotic systems if he can. It may well be that the device is in a position where it's not accessible to a robot. He'll try to neutralise the device from a stand-off distance so he's not hazarding himself or any member of his team. But at some stage, he's going to have to go forward and actually do something with the device. He'll take a series of steps before he does that; protecting himself using his search team to eliminate threat and electronic countermeasures to eliminate other forms of threat. But at the end of the day, he's got to go forward and he'll go forward *alone*, in order to deal with that specific device.

As he closes in on the area, that's when he's at maximum hazard. The terrorists or insurgents may have set up what we call a 'come on job', deliberately designed to bring people into that location where they may have seeded other IEDs. That's when the operator is at maximum risk. So he needs to go forward very carefully and watch where he puts his feet. Because some of these devices are incredibly difficult to find. Having rendered the device safe, he will recover items of forensic interest; if it's a new type of device it will be of keen interest to the weapons intelligence organisation. They'll want to track where the technology's come from and do something about interdicting the international lines of supply.

Ultimately, the British philosophy is based on trying to either neutralise the device or destroy it. In some situations we want to neutralise the device to recover it completely for forensic evaluation. In other circumstances, we'll just want to destroy it. The difficulty is, you can't just destroy everything you come across because you don't know where the components are. I'm quite often asked why we don't just blow the devices up. Well you know, if we could, we probably would. But actually when things are buried in the ground, you've got to have some idea about where the various device components are. So it's a mix and match. I would certainly not criticise an operator for destroying an IED. If he was under pressure or was losing light, then actually destroying that device would be exactly the right thing to do. And of course that would pose fewer hazards than to go forward and try to get the device out of the ground or start chopping wires. Walking forward and chopping wires is never a good idea. Don't try that one at home.

I think without doubt, during my 27-year career in the army, the most difficult time for me personally was when I spent a lot of time in Afghanistan during the last half of 2008 through to 2010 when we took a lot of casualties. It started with the death of Warrant Officer Gary O'Donnell GM and Bar in the autumn of 2008. Whilst I was out in Afghanistan in 2009 a number of people I knew well were killed or sustained grievous injuries. I was involved in the follow-up technical investigations on a number of these incidents and a couple in particular really brought it home to me, the true reality of the work that we do. After the bombing of the Grand Hotel in Brighton in 1984, the Provisional IRA issued a statement saying, 'Today you have been lucky, remember you need to be lucky always, we have to be lucky only once.' In bomb disposal we too need to be lucky always and each operator only has a finite amount of luck. It is only with hindsight that you can truly appreciate the risks that you have taken during a career in bomb disposal. I think I've been lucky, I know many that have sustained both physical and mental scars as a result of this work. I know many decent families that have also lost their loved ones. What keeps me going is the thought of how many innocent lives that have been saved.

The thing that I miss about the army is those people that I worked with. I think they do a fantastic job. I've got the utmost respect for what our young people are doing in Afghanistan at the moment and they've got my sincere thanks for a job well done. They're outstanding.

STORY TOLD BY COLONEL S.

Captain Lisa Head was the first female bomb disposal officer to be killed. While working on disabling an IED, two hidden devices exploded, one only partially but the second caused fatal injuries. Three more low metal content bombs were found nearby. A senior defence source said: 'It was a classic "come on" ambush. The high metal content IED was put there to be discovered and the low metal content bombs were designed to take out the counter-IED operator.'

(*The Telegraph*, 31 January 2012)

The 'pigstick' (named from hunting wild boar with a spear) is a British Army name for the water-jet disrupter used on the Wheelbarrow robot against the IRA in the 1970s. It fires an explosively propelled jet of water to disrupt the circuitry of a bomb and disable it. The modern pigstick is a very reliable device and is now used worldwide. It was invented in 1972, prior to which bombs were dismantled by hand, which was obviously very dangerous.

THE BUSH PILOT

Extreme rating: ☠☠☠☠☠
Danger level: ▁▁▃▄■■□□□□
Criteria: Commercial pilot's licence and instrument rating; bush pilot course; minimum 500 flying hours
Skills: Bush flying; adaptability; meteorology; people skills; first aid
Salary: £25,000 (US $39,000)

Mentally, I suppose, I have been flying since I was ten.

When I was growing up I wanted to be a pilot with the RAF – that was my goal. I did actually get into the RAF to be a navigating officer but I really wanted to be a pilot so I came out again. I had one of the shortest military careers in existence! All of my flying has been in small aircraft; bush operations. It's the bee's knees, really.

I remember reading a book called *Jungle Pilot* about the life of a missionary pilot, Nate Saint, who was killed in an incident in Ecuador in the 1950s. That story made such an impression on me – my dream was to do that, to be a jungle pilot, never actually realising that I'd end up flying for the same organisation, MAF (Mission Aviation Fellowship). In fact, fairly recently there was a publicity campaign for recruitment with a photo of myself on a float plane in Bangladesh saying, 'Could this be you?' I remembered reading that book and never in a million years thinking that I would actually be doing that. It's thrilling. There I am living the dream. Quite often when I give a talk to children I will ask them – what is your dream? Too often we squash those dreams. It's nice to think that what you wanted as a youngster can come to fruition.

My dream was to have a Land Rover and a plane and in Tanzania my dream came true! I had an old colonial bungalow and at the bottom of the garden, so to speak, a Land Rover and two planes: my toys. A Cessna 210 – my long distance sports car – and a Cessna 206 – my aerial Land Rover.

I love flying for many reasons: the four stripes on the shoulders; the way they call you commander in some countries; the difference you can make to a lot of people using a large piece of aluminium; being part of a team that extends from Guernsey to New Zealand; the fact that everyone looks up at you (pun intended) and fulfilling a boyhood dream.

The variety is tremendous. We support a lot of organisations and fly to 2,500 airstrips around the world with a fleet of over 135 aircraft operating out of 30-plus countries. We mainly operate in Africa, South America and some Asia-Pacific countries including the Northern Territory in Australia.

It's often a partnership. For instance, we do the blood run in Uganda in conjunction with the blood bank, taking screened blood up and bringing unprocessed blood back. It's just something that goes on month in, month out.

You have to do a bush flying course to get experience operating in tricky conditions and I did mine for six weeks in Scotland. It was great flying up there, using the small dirt runways and grass strips; flying out to Coll and Mull in the islands and up the valleys – just great. The aircraft we had was relatively low powered so that mimicked the hot and high flying we have in Africa. It was a very demanding course and it really did sharpen my skills.

Bush flying demands flexibility. Things are not always quite what they seem. If you fly into Gatwick, for instance, it probably hasn't changed since the last time and if it has, you get a note and some paperwork, whereas with bush flying we have to keep up with the conditions – for instance rain can change an airstrip. So if you are in the Sudan with its black cotton soil, it may be fine on the surface but if you break through, it's sticky and you'll decelerate very quickly and have difficulty taking off. So an airstrip that was OK when you last went can become a problem if it's the rainy season, or if trees or grass have grown very quickly since you were last there. Before now I have had to cut down saplings with my Swiss Army knife. You can't be an MAF pilot without one!

The strip can change. Sometimes you can't land. You have to make the decision – is this safe? Can I land here? I always say that any idiot can land a plane anywhere in the world, but only pilots can take off again! We'll fly over if we're not sure, do a low pass or touchdown and feel the wheels; if we still aren't certain we go round again.

You have textbook flying – what should happen – but sometimes it's not quite as is, so you might choose to leave two passengers behind, try take off and if it works, come back for them. You have options like that. It's the need to be adaptable. Yes, we follow systems and a strict rule book but there are times when you have to go with what's actually in front of you. I think that's what makes it such a great job. It evolves very much from day to day.

The other thing, of course, is that you get to know your passengers and the locals.

I had one trip some years ago to visit the Karamojong warriors in north-east Uganda; a tribe whose cattle are everything and which they protect with home-made rifles and AK47s. I'd flown in some medics – Baptist missionaries who were holding a clinic at this cattle camp – and I stayed with them for a couple of days. It was incredible; there was a real rodeo feel. There were warriors armed to the teeth guarding the cattle, young female camp followers, flies everywhere, men firing their guns in the air every morning, and scouts walking out, setting up the route for the cattle. It was a privilege to be part of it.

Even now they have lots of cattle raiding and it's still an issue. I was landing in Moroto recently and there had obviously been some hassles because a tank just rolled out across the runway. I was thinking, *I don't suppose that should be there really*. So I overflew it, came back and landed. They do have trouble, but generally it's friendly.

I stay with the local folk. They are not just being nice. They figure if they have the pilot you can't leave without them!

Just a few weeks ago I was in south Sudan staying in an African hut and we were sitting outside chatting. They were telling me how in the previous week they'd had a storm come through that was so violent it set fire to some of the village huts. A few people had been killed. Three of them went out to help. The two that were left heard AK47s rapidly firing and thought they were under attack but the locals were just firing at the storm.

It's that variety of people.

There's no fear of the planes. Most of the folk out there are smart enough to realise that the whirling thing could ruin their day and so they generally keep out the way of the propellers. There is a respect for them. But what often happens is that you get crowds and you have to be careful with a large number – particularly children on some airstrips. They are probably the biggest hazard. In Bangladesh I could draw a crowd of 5,000 people. It's a huge occasion just watching a float plane land.

Another hazard is that you get animals on the runways. Goats are the worst because unlike other animals which scatter, goats panic and say 'group huddle!' and they all run together. Once I was on a strip in Mozambique and I had to clear the runway by doing a low pass because there was this guy riding down it on his bike. To this day I'm still mystified – I must have whipped past his head at 100 knots and made him levitate off his bike!

I have had some problems with the locals carrying spears and bows and arrows. On the small aircraft – the 206 – we are fine because they can't fit their spears underneath the wing. But on the Cessna Caravan you really have to watch that because they gesticulate with their hands and spears and could easily do some damage. I have to shout at them very firmly to get away from the wings.

On one occasion they had bows and arrows and as I was waiting for a passenger I thought I'd have a go. I'm no Robin Hood but the first shot hit the target! Then they all had a go and not one of them hit it! This is bad news; this is about face saving now. So I had another go and was nowhere near and eventually, after many tries, one of them hit the target. It was quite interesting because they bounce the arrow. I think they do this to try and hit an animal from underneath. They bounced the arrow in front and were able to hit the target this way and I was able to make a big fuss. Honour was restored.

A couple of weeks ago I was walking an airstrip and I found this huge hole and a live mortar round. I often wonder how it could have got onto the airstrip.

We frequently have to do medivacs (medical evacuations) and we are trained in first aid. Sometimes we just pick up walking wounded and take them on the shuttle flight. I remember in western Uganda, there was a little girl with kidney failure. She had been picked up by some doctors who thought they may be able to save her. I remember parking the plane and there were these tsetse flies… nasty. The plane was under attack and there was this ping, ping, ping, ping as they hit the aircraft. It was the fastest loading I've ever done because I'd been flying a float plane all day and I was wearing shorts!

And although the little girl died, the mother asked, 'Why did you bother?' and I think that sums up a lot of our work. We can bother and make a difference.

We used to fly a lot into the north-eastern corner of Tanzania to a hospital strip right on a ridge in Murgwanza. It was an interesting one, a fairly short runway, so we had to push the plane back until the tail touched the fence – that extra 6 inches was vital. And then when you took off there was a bend in the airstrip and if you went too fast you couldn't quite get round it; you had to be at just the right speed. And while you always aim to take off, technically you didn't need to because the ground just plummeted away at the end so you instantly had a couple of thousand feet below you. Once you had committed you couldn't abort. There are many airstrips like that, that are less than ideal. We always pray a blessing before we take off!

It's a technically skilled job with lots of variety. I enjoy it.

The float flying is the most demanding and exciting. You really do have a thousand airstrips before you; it's so versatile. I was flying in south-eastern Bangladesh, there was a storm ahead and I saw lightning strike the ground ahead of me, so I just looked around, saw a nice bit of water and landed, dropped anchor. No one would have seen a plane there before, it was just a random bit of water. But I remember there was a meadow and all these people meandered down the paths and waded into the water. I have this image of these groups of families up to their necks in water just standing looking at me, fascinated with their umbrellas up as the rain cascaded down while I just sat in the plane waiting for the storm to pass.

I have to say it is a very privileged job. It's challenging, fun, a job you dream about – to have a Land Rover and an airplane in your backyard and to be operating in the bush. You are independent and free. You are often flying to areas where few people ever go.

There is a sense of adventure.

I remember flying out nine female South African hearing therapists once – they were all pretty and blonde – and as I walked through the airport with a train of them behind me, I was thinking: it doesn't get much better…

It's often the unexpected that catches you out. There was a 4,265-feet long hand-dug channel through a swamp and we had a float plane there. On one of my first flights I taxied down the channel and got caught in some reeds. To get going again you have to get someone to hold the stern against the bank, get the engine started, add a lot of power and then launch forward. So we were in this channel against the shore with a guy holding the plane, I added power and slowly went off but I couldn't hold the course. What had happened was he had got caught up in the rope and I was pulling him along the channel in the water!

Sometimes I would take a local newspaper to the police on the remoter islands of Lake Victoria – it's brilliant going out there! Once I was taking off and I heard a strange noise over the engines: something wasn't right. So I looked back and there was this guy – a few sandwiches short of a picnic – hanging onto the tail stinger, grinning his head off, and I was dragging him through the water. So I turned round and 300 feet off shore he let go and swam.

Some people are on really remote stations. Just taking the papers or passing the time of day with them for five minutes can make the difference to their sanity. There are some amazing people out there. I think I have the easy job; it's the people you are working with and the five minutes on the ground which give you the magic.

STORY TOLD BY BRYAN

In 1956, Nate Saint and four other missionaries (Jim Elliot, Ed McCully, Peter Fleming and Roger Youderian) were killed in Ecuador by the Waorani (Auca) Indians they had come to support. The tribe – known for their unprovoked killing sprees – attacked them with spears on the beach.

Bush flying often involves using float planes as they allow for flexible landing sites. They have two floats whereas flying boats use their actual fuselage as a giant float to land with. The most famous flying boat was the 'Spruce Goose'; the largest flying boat ever built with the longest wingspan of any aircraft. Designed by the recluse Howard Hughes, it had a massive 322-foot wingspan. It only flew once: 1 mile on a test flight.

THE FORMULA ONE DRIVER

Extreme rating: ☠☠☠☠☠
Danger level: ▁▁▪▪◼◼◼◼☐
Criteria: Immersion experience practising, training and winning in karting, Formula 3000, Formula 3, test driving, etc. very useful from an early age; consistent natural talent; physical fitness; technical competence; a lot of money or a team/sponsorship package
Skills: Mental toughness; courage; determination; competitive instinct; quick reactions; precision analysis
Salary: £13.8 million (US $21.5 million) in 2011 for the highest paid driver, not including endorsement money

British Grand Prix, Brands Hatch, 1974. I was there and that was when I knew I wanted to be a Formula One driver. That was the day that the hairs on the back of my neck stood up. The noise was amazing. The whole show set me alight. I was ten.

My uncle used to run a kart track in St Ives and I spent maybe three days a week down there flying around and beating everybody; then he bought an old kart and it became a family thing at weekends to go to Tilbury Docks and race. As soon as I got in the kart, I was at one with it. The 'natural' instinct came out straight away. There was no fear.

You can't have fear because it will hold you back. It doesn't matter if it's braking, turning, sliding the kart… no different than Formula One: it needs the same mentality to push it to the limit. You have to be on the edge of the track and you have to be within an inch of the limits to get the maximum out of the car. If you don't go to the limit, someone else will go faster. That's what drives you: the competitiveness with the other guys on the track and the competitiveness within you. You're always trying to beat, first of all, yourself, and then trying to beat them – especially your teammate who's in the same car as you. You are the one who's got to get perfection out of the car. You know where it needs to be on the track. And it's about utilising your engineers and designers to make the car work in a way that you need it to, to be able to produce the best speed out of it.

In the back of your mind, in a very deep, locked, dark little place of your brain, maybe there is the fear. But it will stop you. The successful drivers who get to Formula One don't have that fear. They have belief.

I've never had a perfect lap. You get close to it now and again. I don't think even Michael Schumacher's had the perfect lap or even the perfect corner. You might have a good race, from lap one to lap seventy-three, but that doesn't mean it's perfect. There are other factors that come into play – strategy, tyres, what to do when the weather changes… There's the mental side of it as well, not just the physical. Being confident that you're going to beat everybody else.

Before my accident, I believed that I could beat anybody, anywhere, anytime, any track, any condition. After my accident, I lost that. I never had that feeling again. I had it, I had the accident, and then I lost it. Lewis Hamilton and Sebastian Vettel have utter belief in themselves. They're young and have been groomed from an early age. They absorb it all in. They suck in the energy, and then they channel it.

After my accident, in my head I still thought I could do it. If I hadn't had that, I don't think I'd have tried as hard to get over the injury, to get back. And I think some people would have given up. The pain's too much.

I still remember in the hospital being able to move my foot 1 millimetre. It was pathetic really, but I used that negative and turned it into a positive. Because I had to. I wanted to. It strengthened me.

I had to laugh about it; that was the only way I could get over it. If I was too serious, it would have fried my brain, burnt me out. I had to laugh. It was my way of releasing the issues that I had. I couldn't share everything with people, not even my wife. My right toe got partly cut off and stitched back together, and for the last 20-odd minutes of a race, it used to absolutely kill me, but I couldn't tell anyone because they would have thought, 'He's got a problem there. Move him out.' So I had to have the mental strength not to tell anybody and deal with it myself. You've got to be strong. You've got to use all the energies around you in a positive manner. You channel them.

You have to be very, very driven and very, very focussed. Partly because there is so much technology involved nowadays, which takes up a lot of mental capacity. You've got all these engineers, computers, wind tunnels and simulators, and they all have to be taken into account to enable you to get yourself in the best position to win. There's only three weeks testing now, the rest is all done in the simulator.

With Vettel, you don't see any cracks in his armour at the moment. He makes mistakes for sure, but he makes way less mistakes than everybody else. He's almost, at the moment, the perfect driver. He's fantastic out of the car, he's fantastic with the team, and he's fantastic when he's in the car as well. Vettel is probably the first 'almost' full product that we've seen.

I like Button and Hamilton. They've got different mentalities. Lewis is of the age. He's on the edge, and it's fantastic to see, but he makes far too many mistakes. It's mental, totally mental. Jenson's more controlled. He used to be quite a party boy. I think he probably still is in his way, but it's very controlled now, where it wasn't before.

I think Frank Williams told him to change. He comes across brilliantly, really professional, and I'm pleased for him. He's in the right place.

The best year that I had was with Mika Häkkinen at Lotus in 1991–92. I'd go quicker, then he'd go quicker, then I'd go quicker. The whole weekend and the whole two years that we were together were like that, because we were battling each other. And it was brilliant. I look back and I did enjoy it, because we were really competitive and we got on really, really well. But then, in the latter part of the relationship, it started to change because the competitiveness got so strong that we didn't talk to each other. We knew that we couldn't because it was down to us beating each other. But it was great. It was my most intense rivalry with a teammate because we were so close. And we'd learn off of each other. I had two years of that, and it was really good.

I can see people like Senna and Prost having the same thing. They're learning off of each other, watching each other, trying to utilise what they've got but also what the other might have. You try to find out what they're doing, and there are games of waiting around for them to have another cup of tea, so you can compare notes. It's one-upmanship. You're trying to beat your teammate at the end of the day. You've got the same car and you want to get yourself to a number one position, to become the world champion.

My most successful season was '95, when I came fourth in the World Championship, but I wouldn't say it was my best year. My problem was with Flavio Briatore who was running the team, because whatever my teammate – Michael [Schumacher] – wanted, he got. So that was mentally my toughest season, because I was on my own in some regard. I didn't have the backing of a team manager. I got on well with Michael, I still do today, but you knew it was always about him. I had to adapt the best I could. I knew it was going to be Michael's team, I probably just didn't realise how strong he was; it was always about him and him alone. And that's why he was as successful as he was.

You've got to have the edge. You've got to get the power, but I'd say 95 per cent of it is mental. You can't rest on your laurels because F1 moves on so damn fast, you've got to be on top of it the whole time, which Michael was very good at doing. From the very beginning of day one, he was on top of it. Other drivers weren't.

Driving perfectly every single lap, every race, every session, every season, is bloody hard. There is no relaxing. It's a bit like a 100-yard sprint, from start to finish, for two hours, with Mike Tyson giving you a smack in the face every five seconds. Which is why motor racing drivers are some of the fittest if not *the* fittest of sportsmen, because they have to contend with a lot of different things: mentally, physically, in the car, out of the car.

Much of the mentality of the new generation – let's call it a strong desire to achieve – is in the sacrifices. And they all sacrifice. They have their fun times off-season, but it's for a very short time. It might be once, maybe twice during that off-season, but if you do that too often, you won't succeed.

Early in my career I got the buzz as soon as I arrived at a track. Latterly, no; I assume because I have the experience and gotten used to it. The nerves would come about an hour before the race, in the build-up. Early on, it was more intense: wanting it, very, very hungry for it. And then latterly, the same thing – you're still hungry for it, still wanting it – but you get into the routine, you know what to expect.

It was always intense and it was always non-stop. If you go into a paddock these days, you'll never see a driver because they're going from the car to the motorhome to a sponsorship meeting, back to the track, discuss the car, in the car, out of the car, analysing… it's non-stop. There isn't time to relax. I remember when I was with Michael at Benetton, about an hour before the race we both had a lie down and a sort of mini-kip. That was nerves.

The plan is to get the best start you can, and deal with whatever's going on in front of you, then get into a rhythm: tyres, engine, monitoring what's going on, a little bit of discussion with the team (but not much). There's no plan as such. If you're at the front, you've got to get the best start, get to the corner first and then get into the rhythm straight away. Hopefully then all the work you've done has given you a car that you're able to drive at 100 per cent for the whole race and that's enough to keep you in front of all the guys behind you. It's just getting that first lap, or first corner, out of the way. Once that's done, then it's down to rhythm and balance.

We had a time when you could go flat out for 15 laps, come in, pit stop, new tyres, flat out for another 15 or so laps. It was just flat out, flat out. Fantastic – very different – but there was no thought process. I like it now, where the driver has to monitor how the tyres are and react to that. With all the data that we analyse, there is a big difference between everything that goes before the race and everything that happens in the race. There are many times when the tyre companies say, 'You can't use that tyre, because it's shown to wear X amount' beforehand, but in the race it will be completely different. You're driving differently, the conditions are different, the tyre will react differently. So sometimes you have to try and think beyond that, because things change. It's balancing risk and strategy. If I'm doing the same as the four cars in front, how am I going to overtake them and go quicker? A riskier strategy normally works out, but that's when you're further down the field. If you're at the front, it's different; it may be about having a safer strategy.

I go as fast as I can. It's the limit, and the limit is the limit. Monaco is the prime example of speed. It's not a high-speed track by a long, long way; the average is 88 miles per hour, compared with Silverstone at 157 miles per hour, but the speed difference is sort of immaterial to us. It's not about the maximum speed we go down the Monza Straight for example (220 miles per hour), or Monaco (215 miles per hour); it's the speed that you can go from the point you brake to the point you're on the throttle. *That* is the challenge. It's not the bit in-between. It's not: you brake, you change gear, you turn, you hit the apex, you drift out. It's got to be one movement effectively. And that's why I say it's very hard to get it perfect. The speed can be 40 miles per hour, or 150 miles per hour, the challenge is to get it absolutely as fast as you can; the speed is immaterial.

When I race, on my first lap, I will be doing my best. On my second lap, I will be wanting to do better than the one before. Every lap has to beat the lap before. That was my way of concentrating. I literally went into a rhythm and then I would achieve the consistency as well. Consistency in racing is almost the most important thing. Speed, yes, you've got to have the speed, you've got to be right on the edge, but consistently. And that's the hardest thing to do. It's mental and physical at the same time.

So all those elements need to be there. I see it like a jigsaw: one piece missing, and you're a million miles away. You'll struggle. The harder you try, you'll keep taking another piece away. It's a rhythm, and it's about controlling yourself.

Driving in the rain is like driving down a wet motorway behind a truck. You can see its lights, but you can't see left. You can't see right. It's exactly the same, except everyone's going the same way, so from that point of view, you generally know nothing's going to come towards you. One of the worst wet races I did was in Australia in 1991. We drove just 14 laps and they stopped the race. The only way you could drive, because you could see nothing in front, was by using your peripheral vision. You could only really judge where you were on the track by the barrier. Sometimes you couldn't even see that. But your instinct is not to back off. You know that if you do, either someone might drive in to the back of you or you're going to lose out. So you can't do that.

THE FORMULA ONE DRIVER

I like the challenge of racing in the rain, I like being on the edge. You've got to react quickly. Generally motor racing drivers have hugely fast reflexes so you can control the car in the wet. It doesn't happen all the time; people do spin of course. It's a challenge, and I don't mind that. There were bits where you could see absolutely sod all. You might see a bit of barrier, you might suddenly see a light in front of you, but you'd react. It wasn't the nicest of feelings because you didn't know what was going on around you, absolutely nothing, but I liked it. It was the thrill of not knowing. I never had a problem racing in the wet.

What happened with Massa's accident was freaky. The chances of a spring falling off one car, bouncing straight down the track and then end up at a trajectory the same height as his head. You can't do anything about that. There's talk about putting tops on the cars like a fighter jet canopy, they've been looking into it. But if you rolled over, you wouldn't be able to get out.

All the issues, pressures and, sadly, the deaths we've had over the years – you can only improve safety to a certain point. You can't stop absolutely everything and you've got to be lucky. It doesn't matter which sport – rock climbing, mountaineering, base jumping, bobsleigh... same thing. They're still learning. F1 safety is not a complete and utter 100 per cent science yet.

Like it says on the programme: 'Motorsport is dangerous.' You don't know if you're going to have a clean race. You do everything you can to make it safer, and then some freaky little thing can happen. In motorsport where there is a death, it's very hard to be ahead of the game. Every accident, every incident, is different. Sadly, you learn from the bad ones.

When I had my big accident at Brands Hatch in 1988, I hit the barrier head-on and the whole of the front of the car exploded back to my knees. Then it spun round, went across the track and unfortunately head-on in to the barrier again with my legs hanging out the front. So they got pushed in. When it stopped and I opened my eyes and looked down, there was just a big hole in the front; I thought I'd lost my legs from the knee down. I couldn't see my feet.

Then I remember a marshal running up, and he backed away looking worried. It was one of those things. Just bloody unfortunate. It was all happening for me one minute and suddenly it all shattered.

Although in my eyes, it hadn't. That was the thing. When I eventually came round in intensive care, I never thought, 'That's it. It's over.' I never, ever thought of giving up. It was always, 'I'm going to get back, I'm going to drive, I'm still going to be a racing driver.' And down the line that did work out. Bloody painful.

When I got to the first race after my crash, in Rio, no one was expecting anything. I couldn't really walk; they used to lift me into the car. My left foot was still very swollen and there was one particular bump on the track that when I went over it, in practice and qualifying, it killed me. It was like someone got a knife and stabbed my ankle. It hurt like hell. And it would take ages for the pain to go away, but then I'd come around for the next lap, and it would bump again. What I learned to do over the weekend was relax my leg as I came up to the bump, it'd hit the bump, my foot would smack up on the side, it would hurt like hell, and then I got over that pain threshold. So for the actual race, it wasn't a problem. It was really bizarre. I finished fourth. That saved my career.

I remember the crash. Does it bother me? No, it happened so quickly. A very short bang that sort of echoes and spreads. When you're in it, it's just so bloody quick. I remember shooting across the track, turning sideways, a lot of head movement forward, a bit of spinning, another head forward... I can vaguely remember feeling, 'S***, this is going to be big.' I had no time to even think. And no feeling of pain, no feeling at all.

Before it happened, I thought, it can't happen to me, but it did. I got over it. Started racing again, and thought it won't happen to me again. It could do. I know that. I still know it. But again, that's part of this psychological thing… if you think something's going to happen, yes it is. It's a belief that you're in control of your destiny.

STORY TOLD BY JOHNNY

In 1994 there were two deaths on one black F1 weekend at Imola.

Ayrton Senna was leading the race when he slewed off the track at 190 miles per hour and hit a concrete wall. Professor Sid Watkins, head of the medical team reported:

'He looked serene. I raised his eyelids and it was clear from his pupils that he had a massive brain injury. We lifted him from the cockpit and laid him on the ground. As we did, he sighed and, although I am totally agnostic, I felt his soul departed at that moment.'

A rookie in F1, Roland Ratzenberger died a day earlier at the same race. His car crashed into a wall at 196 miles per hour. The impact was so strong that it broke his neck.

To date:

- Michael Schumacher is the most successful driver of all time with 91 wins.
- The fewest number of finishers in one race is three – Monaco 1996.
- Highest top speed – Juan Pablo Montoya in 2005 reached 231.52 miles per hour.

THE GRAND NATIONAL
JOCKEY

Extreme rating: ☠☠☠☠☠
Danger level: ▄ ▄ ▄ ▄ ▄ ▄ ▄ ☐☐☐
Criteria: Right weight and build; physically fit; National Hunt racing (horse racing over jumps) experience or apprenticeship
Skills: High level of skill, empathy and understanding in riding and handling horses; fitness, strength and stamina; determination and dedication; good judge of pace; good eyesight and fast reaction speeds; ability to cope with the risks and pressures of racing; knowledge of horse care and welfare
Salary: £100,000 (US $156,000) average

I came from a broken home – there wasn't much love in any of the houses I lived in – but I found I had an affinity with horses. There was one nearby on a local farm and I spent all my time out of the house enjoying myself… just good old fun on the farm. I started riding a friend's horse and worked part-time in a local riding stable at weekends and it went from strength to strength. I worked in a laundry before school, folding up sheets, to keep a pony that I had on loan – which my parents had no idea about.

I was 14 and academically unsound. My art teacher at school introduced me to a racehorse trainer in Andover, Toby Balding, who straight away looked at my hands and said, 'You're gonna be too small to be a National Hunt jockey, but there is a top trainer in the country, Captain Ryan Price (who was an ex-commando, a top man in World War Two) who is training at Findon, near Worthing.' He made an introduction and I was set up with an apprenticeship there, for flat racing.

I'd watched Red Rum win the Grand National. I remember this horse was a household name. And I loved jumping, although I was very small. I weighed 6½ stone when I was 16, which is the right weight for a flat race jockey. So I signed up for an apprenticeship which only paid £2.50 (US $3.90) a week back in the 1980s but I loved every moment of it. We'd start at five in the morning and work every hour that God sent looking after horses. I progressed from being a stable lad very quickly to knowing that I had to be a jockey. I realised I didn't want to be shovelling s*** all my life and looked for bigger things; I had a true belief that I was going to become a National Hunt jockey and ride in the Grand National even though I was so small.

I went on from there and managed to have some rides on the flat for the captain. By the time I was 18, I'd already put on nearly 2½ stone and had grown very quickly – shot up – and then it became apparent that I wasn't going to be a flat jockey; my love was for the jumping. Captain Price had five jumping horses and 90 flat horses. Sunday would be their schooling day and I'd wait back – even on my weekends off – hanging around the stable trying to get a ride on a horse that was jumping. And it happened. I jumped a lovely, big steeplechase horse called Broad Lees. Then a flat jockey told me there was a jump jockey's job going in Epsom; and I took it and went to ride for a chap called Arthur Pitt, where I had my first National Hunt rides.

My first horse was called Sign Center Again and was very closely placed in a novice hurdles at Fontwell. He ran very well. I knew straight away that this was where my life was going to be, with the National Hunt fraternity. I liked the people, I loved the horses and still to this day have a lot to do with them. I took on a lot of different freelance National Hunt jobs riding for several different trainers. When I had ridden in only five races I called the top trainer in the country to see if I could ride his horse in the Gold Cup. I was about 19 by then.

It was something I always knew – luckily, because I had nothing else going for me academically. I couldn't focus in the classroom; I always wanted to be at the stable. I knew from day one what I was going to be. My drive for it was so strong. I'd just sleep, eat and talk horses from morning to night.

I started to get a lot of rides. I was placed in the junior championship as a conditional jockey. Jockeys start with a claiming weight from the horse's back, and I started as a 7-pound claimer and got a lot of rides. When you're claiming 7 pounds from the horse because you're younger and lighter, you're well worth your weight in gold and I managed to get a lot of very good horses to ride. I rode through four seasons without an injury. And then the injuries started; it's inevitable. One in ten horses fall and one in ten of those falls are usually quite nasty. Once a month you're probably kicked around on the ground. I broke my collarbone 14 times.

In a season I would do three, four hundred races. And there was one fall I remember still today. It was very early on in the season and I was riding a horse called Fire Drill and he tipped up – just an easy fall – and I was walking back in from the last fence when the owner ran over and slapped me on the back and said, 'Are you OK?' And I thought I was fine, but I hadn't realised I'd snapped my collarbone. And then it never really healed.

Broken bones… 14 collarbones! I have a false ankle now. I had six and a half days in a coma. I broke my neck; I was three months in traction at Addenbrooke's. But I still had the drive. I never lost the will to live. Never lost the drive to ride. There are a hell of a lot of injuries and bouts of concussions, which are part and parcel of being a National Hunt jockey. But every time you hit the floor, you still think you can get up and win the next race. I rode again three years ago for charity and I still had that same thrill and drive… until I turned the top corner at Plumpton where I had my last accident. I had a flashback to that, because I hadn't ridden for 10 or 12 years.

I was lucky to get the ride in the Grand National. I'd won for the owner of the horse before and he'd booked a top jockey who became injured, so I took the ride. The National is a great race to ride in – it's electrifying. There's 100,000 people watching and millions on the television and you do 800 autographs and take a group of public around the track. You can imagine the whole thrill of it.

There are 40 runners in the Grand National. It was amazing. I was quite young – reasonably inexperienced at that level. There was a group of jockeys that were all around the same age. We'd had a very good season and were thrilled to ride in this race. I was picked up by helicopter, flown there with a top trainer, put up for the night and then shipped into the races in the morning.

I don't think I thought I'd made it… I couldn't take it all in. The race was overwhelming. When I came back from the race; that was when it sunk in. I sat and really couldn't believe I'd done it; I just sat overwhelmed. Because it is such a great thing. It's a household name, isn't it? The Grand National. It's a thrilling thing.

The shock was the roar – galloping down to the first fence – the roar from the crowds. I remember it being a reasonably windy day and it was like a tunnel of roaring people on either side. And you've got packed stands of 70,000 or 100,000 people. I was never once scared. I always thought my experience would get me out of any problem I ever got into. You have to have that belief. You know, you always felt in times of trouble you could pull certain levers and get out of the situation. Stupidly, I believed that all the way through!

But I didn't have a particularly good horse to ride, Le Bambino. He burst a blood vessel and I pulled him up.

Becher's Brook… I didn't realise it was coming up as we galloped to it the first time round; I think I'd lost count of the fences. There's no time to think at first; you get settled into the race… and then it comes. And when you're in mid-air, it's like looking over the edge of a cliff. It's a long way down. Probably from take-off to landing you're jumping over 30 feet. From the apex of the jump to the landing would be about 15 feet. That's the drop. On a vertical plane, it's about 9 feet down. They have altered these now. They've brought the landings up a lot.

All you have is this will to go forward and stay on your feet. But as you look down, you don't think you're ever going to hit the floor. These horses aren't used to jumping these jumps – just once a year. Then there was The Chair. You can actually drive a Mini into the ditch in front of the fence. And that is a big leap. A big jump. There were a lot of big jumps in those days. I was never frightened. It was just a feeling… you were doing what you wanted to do. Thrilling. Thrilling.

We spend a lot of time driving around the country in the early hours of the morning, sitting on horses before the race, trying to get to know them. And a lot of the time you haven't sat on them before the race. In fact, the horse in the Grand National I hadn't sat on before. The owner/trainer was quite an amateur and a multi-millionaire. He'd built a 10-foot-wide replica of Becher's Brook in front of his manor house to practise with and it looked monstrous. So I went down to school the horse before the National to jump him and I said, 'You'll never get the horse to jump that, you know, he's going to see this big black thing in the middle of the garden.' So we didn't actually jump him beforehand.

You need to train them on smaller, easier fences; you don't go and train a horse over something like Becher's Brook.

In flat racing, you start in the stalls whereas with jump racing it's always behind the tape. It's over a longer distance, so the matter of a couple of feet doesn't make too much difference, whereas a flat race is very, very precise. Also, there are some horses that you need to start towards the back of the field to settle them down. You may be riding over two or three miles – that's quite a long way, galloping – so you need to produce the run at the right time. Some horses have got staying power, so you set off and use that power and keep galloping. Other horses you hold up and then they've got a burst of pace. And you have to judge the pace, that's a serious part of it: understanding what pace and when the horse wants.

When they are racing, horses get their blood up; they're a lot happier in company. They get a herd mentality and there are horses that want to be at the front and horses that want to be at the back. Thoroughbreds are not herd animals, they are horses that we've created over the last 300 years: they're as close to nature as a tomato in Tesco. They're something we're forever designing. But I'd say 75 per cent want to be at the front; they want to be up there, it's natural for them to be at the front of the race.

I like the front runners, these enthusiastic horses. They have got this will to win and you just have to keep saying, 'No, we'll calm down for a while,' and then try and produce the pace at the right time. They love it. They want to do it. You can't bully them into it. It's no good fighting with them. It's a bit of a psychological battle; you can't fight to stop them and you can't bully them into going faster. You meet them somewhere in the middle. You try to meet them as a mate, more than as a rider.

Most of the horses have a will to be in the front but there are a few that are lazier, some of which are the better ones, because they conserve their energy; they're always quite relaxed. The ones that set off all gung-ho are very hard to settle. They're the ones that are tough to win on. It's just give and take with them until they relax behind the bridle and then pick it up at the right time. As they get older and more trained, they do start to settle. They get older and wiser.

You can't ever have the grandeur on your mind; you're kicked around in the mud regularly. There's the Gold Cup and the Grand National end, fantastic – and then you've got the winter down at Taunton, in the deep mud, on a November day: you haven't eaten for two days, you're wearing a silk, galloping around and it's 1°C. So there are both ends of the scale. That end of the scale wasn't the best. Sometimes it was so muddy you would wear three or four pairs of goggles, pulling them down as they got covered in mud, 'cause you'd have the crap kicked in your face every day. And then at the end of the day, you'd be driving home picking bits of grit out of your eyes. But still, the next day, you were desperate to get up and do it again.

The camaraderie between jockeys is unbelievable. We have a respect for each other. We knew how dangerous it is, so we don't make it any more dangerous. You look out for each other. The camaraderie between the jockeys, in and out of the weigh-in room, was next to nothing I've ever seen. I saw a jockey the other day (he's a trainer now) and it was like the old days – you know, you have this certain bond and it lasts forever. I suppose it's a bit like soldiers going to battle. And once you've done that, the minute you meet them again you're back there again, aren't you? Straight back to where you were.

Your aim is to get to the winning post first, always. There were horses you knew weren't quite fit enough and you'd look after them. And some you knew weren't quite good enough and you'd look after them. But you always believed when you got on a horse, you could win. You always had that belief. You had to. There was no thought about, 'Should

I do this…? Is this gonna happen…?' The minute anything like that goes through your mind, you have to give up.

What's in your brain goes down the rein.

I say that to anyone who rides or who I teach. What's in the brain goes down the rein; it *does* transmit to the horse. If you've got any other thought… if you're half worried, the horse will sense it. If you just think, 'I'm going there,' the horse will go there and you have to have that belief. In any riding. Otherwise you put doubt in their mind. A horse is quite a fragile thing and you can put doubt in their mind *very* quickly if you're slightly hesitant.

The way I look at a rider is they are like the conductor of an orchestra: you're up there and you are the boss, you are the driver. You have to have that belief that you're going there; and not 'win at all costs'. You do realise that they are flesh and blood underneath you and they're not to be abused. I would never take the horse beyond its means and if I ever thought that it shouldn't be racing, I'd pull it up. Because I learned from experience. As a young jockey when you hadn't quite got that experience, you ended up on your head and the horse as well. You're risking yourself but, first and foremost, the horse. So you have to have that belief that you're doing the right thing always.

It was the injuries that caught up with me in the end. After I finished racing, I was jumping a young horse and I didn't fall off but it jumped awkwardly and it knocked me out, without having any contact.

In falling off, a man's natural instinct is to roll into a ball and protect the family jewels. I've fallen in front of 15, 20 horses and they've not put a foot on me. Not even touched me. They've all gone over the top; they're quite dexterous with their feet. I did have an incident once at Windsor where I'd fallen, rolled into a ball and there was an amateur in the race, tailed off probably 300 yards behind the last horse. Most professionals would have pulled up by then but this jockey carried on and as I got up and turned around, I walked straight into his horse. He galloped straight over the top of me.

The most dangerous thing is if you have a loose horse. Once I was in front at Plumpton... my last ride, actually. I had a loose horse a length and a half in front of me, and we were going to the fence at the top of the hill, and the loose horse turned in front of me and I T-boned it and that's the last I remembered for quite some time. Probably took me six months to get my memory back.

I got a lot of respect from being a jockey. As I said, I didn't have much going for me but then being a sportsman, taking it seriously, getting very fit... and the thrill of a group of horses going as fast as they can towards the winning line with you in front is incredible. You know, there's a hell of a lot of expensive horse flesh and top jockeys, riding alongside household names: Johnny Francome, Pete Scudamore, Steve Smith-Eccles, Richard Dunwoody. These were all top jockeys of their time and riding with them was a thrill. And you were taken very seriously at a young age. I was very lucky with the owners – I had some good owners. And it was a great time.

You had rich, powerful men who owned the top thoroughbreds at your feet. And they took you seriously and you took them seriously. And that was the thrill of it: the business side and the sporting side – but the sporting side more so.

STORY TOLD BY CHRIS

DANGER FACT:

Horse racing is a dangerous and physical sport where jockeys can incur permanent, debilitating and even life-threatening injuries including concussion, bone fractures, arthritis and paralysis. Eating disorders such as anorexia are also very common as the jockeys have to maintain such low weights.

THE GRAND NATIONAL JOCKEY

Between 1993 and 1996, 6,545 injuries occurred during official races – an injury ratio of 606 per 1,000 jockey years. In Australia it is considered to be the second most deadly job after offshore fishing. From 2002 to 2006 five deaths and 861 serious injuries were recorded.

 EXTREME FACT:

The first National Hunt race on record took place in County Cork in 1752 over a distance of 4.5 miles. The start and finish were marked by the church steeple in each town, hence the term 'steeplechase'. The first official Grand National race (the 'Liverpool Grand Steeplechase') took place in 1839 and also runs over 4.5 miles. In the Grand National, horses jump 30 fences, including The Chair and Becher's Brook. The Chair is 5 feet 2 inches, with a 6-foot-wide ditch and is the only fence to have caused a human fatality in the National's history. Becher's Brook takes its name from Captain Becher who fell there in the first Grand National. Red Rum won the race three times.

THE HART PARAMEDIC

Extreme rating: 💀💀💀💀💀
Danger level: ▁▁▄▄■■□□□□
Criteria: Must be an experienced Health Professions Council (HPC) registered paramedic or IHCD emergency medical technician; an IHCD emergency driving qualification and valid UK driving licence including category C1 and no more than three penalty points; pass the Physical Competence Assessment (PCA) and Ongoing Fitness Assessments (OFA), capability and competency interviews
Skills: Mental and physical resilience; competent and capable of working effectively in hazardous environments; level-headed; motivated; team player; with self-discipline and good communication skills
Salary: £21,176–£27,625 (US $33,000–$43,000)

HART is the ambulance service Hazardous Area Response Team. It started as a result of reviewing disasters such as 7/7, 9/11, train crashes, and so on. In the past, the ambulance service would be confined to what is called the 'outer cordon', waiting to receive casualties brought to them. However, some casualties in the inner cordon needed clinical interventions sooner, to preserve life at the early stages of an incident. Now, HART have paramedics trained to work in hazardous areas and wearing specific personal protective equipment (PPE). We are able to enter the inner cordon alongside other emergency service partners and work safely, giving paramedic treatment to casualties a lot earlier.

There are currently 14 teams in the UK, with each team comprising 42 paramedics and emergency medical technicians. There is a team of six on at any one time. Where I work we have two staff out 24 hours a day in response cars, responding to category A 999 calls, and four back at base ready to respond with a HART capability. If we need more than four, then the other two can go directly to the scene or come back to pick up a specific vehicle.

The definition of a 'hazardous area' is anything from burning or collapsing buildings, explosions, moving water, working at height, chemical spills, CBRN incidents (chemical, biological, radiological or nuclear), mass casualty incidents such as train crashes, urban search and rescue, firearms incidents… areas that ambulance crews in the past have not worked in. For instance, if there is a building that collapses with people inside, our training allows us to go in with the fire service and treat the patients in situ. The fire service would provide access to the casualty and effect the rescue, we provide the medical treatment. We don't do search and we don't do rescue, although we would obviously assist, but we are the medics.

My team has been operational for a year. From day-to-day we go to a lot of building fires and road traffic collisions. We've also had accidents down on the docks, such as when a seaman fell 30 feet into a ship's hold and had probably broken his back. The HART operative tended to the patient down in the hold, stabilised his injuries, secured him into our specialist stretcher, and then the casualty was lifted with the HART paramedic. This enabled him to maintain medical observations and treatment all the way up, managing the casualty's airway and making sure his condition didn't deteriorate.

So that's a good example of a rescue where the HART paramedic was actually in situ with the patient at all times. There have also been instances of people falling down wells, trapped in grain silos, a lot of waterborne incidents… If the patient can't be brought out of the water, for instance they are trapped in a car and injured, then our role is to get in there to treat them. We also attend flooding incidents and can board rescue boats to be taken to where people need medical treatment. For the Cockermouth floods a couple of years ago two HART teams were deployed.

We would also attach to a search and rescue team if somebody is missing. Then, when they find the casualty, we can start medical treatment straight away if necessary.

We spend a considerable amount of time training even before we start operating officially. We do a week with the police including civil response training for CBRN incidents. We spend two weeks doing breathing apparatus training with the fire service, three weeks incident response training with our own training unit, and train with the military for response to hazardous materials (HAZMAT), more CBRN and mass casualty incidents. Then there is a three-week urban search and rescue paramedic course at The Fire Service College where we train to work in confined spaces, tunnels, collapsed buildings, at height and with heavy transportation such as a train crash or multiple vehicle collisions. Then another week water-response training, working in and around fast-moving water for flood or water rescues. We are also constantly training throughout our careers adding new disciplines to our existing skill base.

We are, at the end of the day, still part of the ambulance service and still paramedics, just doing it in a different kit with some slightly different methods. We're a specialist unit. It's quite ground-breaking for the ambulance service; until recently they didn't have this capability; it's very new and it's taken some adjustment. Traditionally, paramedics work in teams of two on an ambulance or one on a response car. We're now working in teams of six and that brings a whole new dynamic to it. There is a command and control structure to the team and at a scene each member has specific roles to perform; however, as teams we work very well together and are constantly watching each other's back. Everybody has so many different skills and many different backgrounds but we all have one common goal and that's to treat the patient a lot earlier than we could before.

A lot of our training is based around mass-casualty incidents. We have different ways of triaging (determining the priority of patient cases) depending on the situation. We will go into the inner cordon, triage and treat the patient before bringing them back to what we call a 'CCP', a casualty clearing point, where they'll be triaged and treated again. As HART operatives we have various levels of triage depending on the situation and all have slightly different parameters. From there, the patient may go through decontamination and have another triage afterwards, before receiving more treatment and going on to a hospital if necessary.

Our vehicles carry enough equipment for mass-casualty incidents and all the teams around the country have done exactly the same training and have exactly the same kit. We can provide mutual aid or call in mutual aid from anywhere in the country if we need to. If a major incident happens somewhere, like a specific terrorist incident, then we may have more than one team working there. We all know how we work and everybody has the same equipment so we'll hit the ground running and work straight away. That is one of the main reasons why HART was established.

We have a range of vehicles and we take whichever one we need for the specific job. We have two 4x4s which are our urban search and rescue vehicles, and one of them always carries the team leader. This vehicle usually arrives on the scene first, and then the 'light equipment truck'. This is the standard equipment carrier that holds our personal protective equipment such as breathing apparatus, gas-tight suits, PRPS (Powered Respirator Protective Suits), working at height equipment and water response kit. It also carries our HART general response kit, like CCP and scene management equipment, DIM (detection, identification, monitoring) equipment which monitors gas levels in the air, all our general medical equipment, mass casualty equipment, a lot of stretchers and a mass-casualty oxygen system.

In addition to this vehicle we have the heavy equipment carrier, which brings all the backup kit. We also have the forward command unit, two response cars and the Polaris. The Polaris is a go-anywhere vehicle, which comes on the back of another truck, stored on a 'pod' which is lowered off the back. It's a six-wheel drive, all-terrain vehicle for taking us to inaccessible areas or inside the inner cordon, carrying us and our equipment in, and bringing patients out. It's handy, especially working around this area because we use it in the New Forest – anywhere that's inaccessible by road. Every vehicle has a 'night owl' – a lighting system on top which puts out a startling amount of light.

We wear incident ground kit, which is our general turn-out uniform. It looks like firefighter clothing, but isn't rated to the same level of thermal protection. It's coloured green to symbolise that we are medics and is designed to protect us in most environments. It zips together, is comfortable and easy to move in, and has a blood barrier membrane to stop any blood coming through onto us. That's one level of kit.

We also wear extended duration breathing apparatus for working in low oxygen environments or where we're not sure what's in the atmosphere. If that's the case, we usually wear a gas-tight suit as well. As the fire service have responsibility for staff entering an inner cordon, our level of PPE will always match theirs. So if they say, 'We're wearing a gas-tight suit and BA,' then we wear a gas-tight suit and BA (breathing apparatus). Then we have powered respirator protective suits, which are a bit like gas-tight suits except they have their own electronic filtration system. It filters toxic agents out and lets clean air in, but you need oxygen in the atmosphere to be able to use them.

The gas-tight suit will not let any gases in whatsoever. The suits are very cumbersome, big, heavy, hot and awkward to work in – not very dextrous. They have thick gloves built into them but we still have to be able to put needles into veins or conduct IO (intraosseous) cannulation, where we drill a hole into the bone to put drugs into the patient. We have to do all our paramedic skills in this kit, give drugs, draw up drugs, control airways, control injuries, control haemorrhage... whether we're around water that's moving fast, whether we're halfway up a crane, or whether we're in a CBRN incident.

All these levels of equipment have certain wear duration as well. We can wear a breathing apparatus for 70 minutes at a time, but if we're wearing it in conjunction with a gas-tight suit, it's only 30–40 minutes because of the environment that we're working in. It gets very hot and sweaty and you have to be very aware of the risk of dehydration. The breathing apparatus weighs 75 pounds, the gas-tight suit weighs 30 pounds, plus you're carrying all your medical equipment, so that's a lot of weight to carry around in difficult environments, and then you have to treat somebody medically while you're wearing it. It can be very demanding.

We also wear a 'bodyguard' system which is attached to our breathing apparatus. We go through a breathing apparatus entry control where there is a telemetry board and one of the team will be tasked as the breathing apparatus entry control officer (BAECO). Their job is an extremely responsible one and this would be their sole tasking. They check you in and then the BA set provides telemetry back to the board about each wearer; what duration they have left in their cylinders, what the temperature is in the area that the wearer is working, what time they went into the scene, what time they are due to come out. We have a whistle that goes off when we get down towards the end of our endurance. That's what we call 'time of whistle'. We can manually send a distress signal to the BAECO, plus it detects motion – so if we haven't moved for 20 seconds, it will set off an alarm which can be cancelled by the wearer. This alarm will send an emergency signal to the BAECO if the wearer doesn't cancel it.

The DIM (detection, identification, monitoring) kit detects oxygen, carbon monoxide, hydrogen sulphide, methane and radiation levels. We also have DIM kit that we can scan over the patient to tell us what level of radiation they may have been exposed to. We have other ones that detect oxygen, carbon monoxide and methaemoglobin levels in the patient's blood.

For water response, we wear drysuits, water rescue/USAR helmets, personal floatation devices and have the choice between two different types of lifejacket. So there are a lot of levels of PPE. We step into all the different disciplines, which is interesting.

A lot of our medical kit – like blast dressings, tourniquets and clotting agents – comes from the military, such as the kit they're using in Afghanistan. The clotting agent is something that you can put into a bleeding wound where it sticks together to form a blood clot, so ideal for gunshots, explosions or big wounds. It looks like a compact toilet roll and we roll layers off and pack it into the wound where it clots the blood and stops haemorrhaging.

We're performing the equivalent of military medicine in a civilian environment. It's got to be effective: life-saving interventions as quickly as possible to stop the bleeding, control the airway, control the breathing, control the circulation, stabilise the patient, get them out and get them to hospital as soon as possible. We are starting the treatment a lot earlier than we could before. That's why HART was established.

STORY TOLD BY C

The Tokyo sarin incident is an example of a CBRN attack in modern times. This killed 13 people.

World War One was described as 'the chemists' war', where tear gas, mustard gas, phosgene and chlorine gas were used, killing 4 per cent of the combatants. In the 1925 Geneva Protocol, the signatory nations agreed not to use poison gas in the future, stating, 'the use in war of asphyxiating, poisonous or other gases, and of all analogous liquids, materials or devices, has been justly condemned by the general opinion of the civilised world.' However, in World War Two precaution was still taken and children and adults were taught to carry and wear gas masks.

One of the earliest known casualty management systems stems from Roman times when aging centurions, no longer fit to fight, were responsible for looking after the wounded – removing them from the battlefield and providing some form of care, suturing wounds and completing amputations.

In the Crusades, the Knights Hospitallers of the Order of St John of Jerusalem had a similar role and this organisation continued, now known as the St John Ambulance.

THE HOTSHOT (WILDLAND FIREFIGHTER)

I'm on a 'Hotshot' crew. After my military service firefighting on structures and aircraft, I decided to try wildland firefighting. I've been two years on the Hotshot crew now which is the elite firefighting team in the US.

We travel around North America, Canada, Alaska and Mexico, wherever there are big fires, and we are tasked with the most difficult jobs. We'll go out there and cut with chainsaws, or burn off fire lines with drip torches, fight fire with fire and we work with helicopters a lot. That's pretty much what we do in a nutshell.

The basic concept is, if you have a huge fire coming towards you and you can't go in there because it's too hot, you drop a fire line (a control line made with fire) when the winds and conditions are in your favour, and that fire goes to the other fire and if all things work well, they contain each other. We use drip torches which are devices used to start fires and controlled burns using fuel which is dripped out the nozzle.

Our smallest fire this year was about five acres and on a fire that size it's pretty much just our crew (the Flathead Hotshots in Montana) that will take the whole fire – 20 of us will put that fire out in a couple of days. Then the biggest fire this year was well over 100,000 acres – so super huge. We were in Alaska and there were 80 Hotshot crews on the fire, 11 helicopters and all kinds of engines. The ones this summer in Arizona and New Mexico had 2,000–3,000 people working on each fire. So they were pretty big.

It gets crazy sometimes.

We sleep rough at the location of the fire. I think this year I slept in a tent for probably about 70 or 80 days of the summer. For us on the Hotshot crew we'll maybe be 6 or 10 miles out in the mountains and they'll fly in some sleeping bags for us so we can sleep up there for a week or whatever. Camping in the woods means you'll be going to the bathroom in the woods and you'll be eating what we call MREs – meal ready eats, which is like military rations. Sometimes you work until 10.30 or 11 p.m. and maybe come back to a big camp where they'll have bathrooms and a caterer with some sort of meal and you sleep there. You usually pass out and don't wake up until someone kicks you!

For me, that's one of the hardest things; not getting any sleep. I'm older than some of these kids who are like 22; I'm 30 and I want to go to sleep! In Arizona we did a shift that was 36 hours long. We worked for 36 hours straight and I was just dying. When we're on fires, we usually work from six in the morning until ten at night. So we're working all day, 16 hours a day; and nobody wants to hear you complain about how hot it is or how much it sucks.

We're pretty freelance. We go all over the country; we went to Alaska, Arizona, Utah, Wyoming, Idaho and Montana this year. You never know where you're going to go.

At the beginning of the season, in mid May, we have what's called 'Hell Week' and basically they put you through hell! It's very tough physically for five or six days with not much sleep. And then you may get a fire assignment and you'll go straight on it right after Hell Week. Sometimes you may go for a week or two without a fire and we'll do physical training every morning for two to three hours, running hills, usually starting off with a 3-mile run and doing weights and cross-training; it's usually pretty fun. You really need to stay in shape.

It's tough, but like anything else, if you do it enough, your body adapts. I think a lot of people don't understand how powerful the body is. If you're hiking every day, for 16 hours, within a few weeks your body doesn't even notice it. It's like anything else, you just do it and then it's not that bad any more.

I was on a saw team this year, just the two of us. One will be sawing and one will be watching out. There's a lot of trees we cut down but they're not like normal trees; they will be half burned out or one will be leaning something crazy and you're having to go in there. A lot of guys get killed cutting trees down so your partner is basically looking out for you. You've got to trust him completely.

You may be sawing all day. We go by tanks of gas [petrol with 2-stroke engine oil]. It takes 40–45 minutes if you're sawing to go through a tank of gas and usually if I go through more than six tanks, I'll pass the saw to my buddy. But if we're doing like four or five tanks of gas a day, we usually saw every other day; I'll saw and then my partner will saw the next day.

On our crew we have a paramedic and two or three EMTs (emergency medical technicians). Last year a guy broke his leg and he was off for the season. I had three or four injuries this year and if I was in a normal job I would have taken some time off. But we don't get paid if we don't work so you'll have a lot of guys with stuff wrapped, or a lot of bandages! It's kinda funny but not really I guess!

If you're hurt or injured you're usually sent up to be lookout. One person will go up somewhere they can see the whole fire and stay in touch with us in case something happens. The reason people get killed is because they're not paying enough attention to the firewall. It will move when you don't expect it to so we'll put a lookout up there and they pretty much sit there all day.

This year I burned my feet twice. One time I burned them so bad I had to sit out for a couple of days. You have to have at least 8-inch-high leather boots because you walk around in hot coals and maybe 6 inches of flame quite a bit. We go through our boots pretty quickly. On the soles is 2-inch thick Vibram – fireproof. A lot of times we are trying to put a fire line in but there's a huge tree on fire that we're concerned might fall on somebody, so we have to go in and cut it down; but the problem if the tree's on fire is there's a lot of coal and heat at the base of it. So you are standing there trying to cut it down and your feet catch on fire. You'll see guys run out and do a little dance – we call it the fire dance. I burned myself pretty good. I had a blister on top of my foot but the boots stayed intact. So they're pretty solid. A lot of us rebuild our boots after a season, maybe take them to a cobbler and they'll repair them. Every night I'll rub my boots with this special oil that keeps the leather more protected with a fire laminate.

All our clothes are made of Nomex. In the forest we wear green Nomex trousers and yellow Nomex tops, a hardhat and sometimes a

Nomex shroud which covers your face and neck. A lot of times in grass fires we'll put our shroud on so our face doesn't get burned and some of the guys have beards and don't want to burn them! And then we wear several different types of gloves and that's our basic personal protective equipment (PPE).

We always have our pack and fire shelter with us too. So if stuff gets really bad you can make yourself into a baked potato.

A lot of people got killed in the last ten or fifteen years by fire running them down and they couldn't escape: so the fire shelter was designed. The thing weighs about 7–8 pounds; it's pretty heavy and you carry it in your pack all the time. If you have to deploy it, there's a couple of handles and you shake it out like a blanket and then it's designed to wrap around you. We call them Shake and Bake. You get inside and hunker down, facing the right direction and then you bunch up with all your buddies to give you even more protection. It's supposed to be able to withstand quite a bit of heat unless it's direct contact so if there's a tree on fire about 10 feet away, you're probably not going to get burned. The bigger problem is whether you have enough oxygen to keep breathing inside. I haven't had to use one yet, and for those who have it's not a pleasant experience. We don't carry oxygen.

It's dangerous, but we've had a good couple of seasons. We had a couple of guys die down in Texas this year but relatively few for this season considering how many hours we worked.

One of the worst things that can happen is that a fire outruns you. Every year we have classes about the fires that have killed people and almost always it's the same combination of things. It may have what we call a light flashing fuel, so really dry grass or shrubs – like in California you have the chaparral which is an oily shrub so it burns really hot and fast. Then the winds will shift or the terrain will be wrong and if all the conditions are perfectly right – or perfectly wrong – the fire will run at 30 or 40 miles per hour. And there's no way you can escape that. Because it's so smoky when the fire's coming towards you, you can hardly breathe anyway. You're not going to burn to death; what will happen is that you'll lose oxygen and pass out and then the fire's going to get you and you don't have a chance.

I've been on a couple of fires where we've called in helicopters; telling them they'd better get there soon or there'll be trouble and they are pretty good about that. On a bigger fire we usually have what's called an Air Attack. It's a fixed wing aircraft and it circles above the fire, watching you and watching the fire. He'll talk to you and you'll tell him where you are exactly and he'll get a couple of helicopters with buckets if need be. If you need to, you just call for a couple of helicopters to come in and straighten you out. We usually use mirror flashes to direct the helicopters in.

I've been hit a couple of times by bucket drops, which is fun!

One of my favourites this summer was when a log fell down across our line and we called in the helicopter. I was standing right over the log telling the helicopter where to come and drop but to let me get out the way first. I start walking away – maybe 20 feet from this thing – and he drops the water on me and doesn't even hit the log that's on fire! There are three basic types of helicopters – Type One, Two and Three. A Type Three can drop about 3,000 gallons of water, so that would really knock you down and could hurt you. The smaller ones carry between 15 and 50 gallons of water and that's more like having a shower. The big ones you wouldn't want to be anywhere near. I've seen them knock trees over.

We see a lot of wildlife but it doesn't really bother us because we're a 20-person crew. We carry bear spray when we're in grizzly bear country, but that's about it. There's mountain cougars from Mexico to Canada, but they're pretty scared of humans so we very rarely see them. They're probably watching all the time but they don't mess with us. I think they are probably a little smarter than bears so they get out of there a lot quicker. These animals have been dealing with fire for thousands of years so they smell it and run the other way. They don't even like campfires.

Way down in Arizona they've got lots of rattlesnakes that bite if you mess with them. Where we are up in Montana the biggest danger is usually a bear in our camp at night. There was a fire last year in Yellowstone and these guys were lighting a fire off the drip torch and a grizzly bear came running out where they were lighting and attacked the guy with the drip torch and then ran off. The bear had totally freaked out and didn't know what to do. We had a lot of grizzlies killing people here this year, so maybe nature's getting mad at us. And then down in California we get what we call 'flaming bunnies', which is kinda horrible. A rabbit or some other small rodent will catch on fire and run across your line and as he's running through the grass he's setting it off and you have to run after these things and try and kill them before they start another fire!

One of the biggest killers is trees falling over – we call them snags. A fire may go through and even when it's completely dead out, there's still all these trees that are either fire-hardened or fire-weakened and they'll stand up straight for years sometimes, sometimes only for days, and if a wind comes through they just fall over. Last year we had two or three people killed by those; this year we've had no deaths, luckily. But that's one of the biggest hazards. So basically it's the fire, the steep country terrain (a guy got hit by a falling rock and broke his leg last year), the snags falling over, the wildlife and definitely some helicopter issues. And driving there. We've had two car accidents as we drive all over the place. I guess there's a list with some of the top ten dangers of the world!

The job I'll never forget is my first fire in 2007. There were about eight or nine of us that almost got killed. We'd just visited a site called

THE HOTSHOT (WILDLAND FIREFIGHTER)

Mann Gulch, one of the most famous early killer fires that killed 13 guys. We'd gone to the site and learned about it; what happened, how they died and the mistakes they made. I then went on my very first fire but as we were driving across the head of it, it cut us off. So we turned around and tried to drive the other way but it cut us off on that side. It's pitch black now; like two in the afternoon and we could hardly see 5 feet in front of us, so we lit off this fire line. The big fire, when it gets big, sucks in all the oxygen, so it sucked our little fire into it. We then drove into the fire we'd just lit off and sat there for about half an hour while 200–300-foot flame lengths were all around us. Pretty crazy. My engine boss was just barking out orders and I appreciate what he did that day. He got some awards and stuff because he saved our lives.

So that was pretty intense.

Sometimes people say to us, 'Oh, that's a really cool picture; that looks pretty crazy'; but they should have been there, because it was a lot crazier than that! You may have 200-foot flame lengths, there's all these helicopters flying around, there's the noise of chainsaws, trees coming down, people barking orders, the radio's blowing up from six different people all yelling at you… No one's shooting at you, but it gets pretty crazy.

I've never been shot at. I had rocket and mortar attacks when I was in Iraq.

The coolest and most unique thing we do is lighting off fire with fire.

We saved a town a few years ago. This huge fire was gobbling up these trees and heading straight for the town and so my boss, Borg, goes to the next mountain over and lights off the entire mountain on fire. You're talking about 5,000–6,000 feet elevation and several miles in diameter. We light off by hand, with drip torches and these guns that can fire several hundred yards, and helicopters dropped fire; so we used all these techniques and lit off this entire mountain. When the helicopters are lighting off with us; that's pretty fun too. They'll drop what we call ping pong balls, which are little white spheres full of glycerine which will light off a fire with you. That's pretty neat. What happened was the mountain pulled the other fire away from the town by sucking in all the oxygen; we saved an entire town by lighting off a whole mountain.

That was pretty cool.

Basically what you are trying to do is, if the fire is moving from right to left, you get on the left side of it and make sure the wind or topography is in your favour (because fire goes uphill and with the wind) and then you light off and they just burn together. We then sit there and watch for what we call 'spots'. When a tree catches fire it will shoot off a whole bunch of embers up into the air. In some fires, it's been known to spot a mile ahead of the fire. And you try to catch all these spots so they don't become bigger fires – you catch them when they are the size of a campfire. That's basically what you are doing when you are lighting off fire. We'll light off roads, we'll light off creek beds, we'll light off rock slopes or cliffs, sometimes we'll put in a line and light off that, so that's the coolest part of the job that I do.

It's the concept of lighting off fire and then the skill with the chainsaws.

We also work with 'smokejumpers' – firefighting guys that jump out of aeroplanes with parachutes; a lot of our guys on the crew are ex-smokejumpers. There's a competition between Hotshots and smokejumpers as to who is tougher. The thing with smokejumpers is they jump out of an aeroplane and they'll put out a small fire, whereas a Hotshot crew is out there for months working almost every single day. They basically do the same job. It's just Hotshots hike there and smokejumpers jump out of planes, so in that regard it might be a little bit more dangerous, but I think we work more.

We are known for working harder, climbing further and going up steeper and crazier slopes than anyone else.

THE HOTSHOT (WILDLAND FIREFIGHTER)

In being dispatched, we sit around what's called the 'cache' – where we go to work every morning before going out on a fire, sharpening our chainsaws and hand tools, pulaskis and stuff like that. Then we get a phone call from dispatch and we're on a two-hour call back, 24 hours a day. So it may be two in the morning, we have to come into the cache and then we drive or fly to wherever we are going. When we get there, we check in with the IC (incident commander) and they will say, 'Hi, you're Hotshot crew, we want you to go and do this' and we'll go in and lay a line, or light off a line, or cut down trees, or fly helicopters or whatever to get the job done. Then when it's all over, we 'demob', go home to our station, sharpen our tools, get our chainsaws ready and wait for the next call.

Usually the IC will give a map out and he'll put some lines in and have some contingency plans. We'll get a weather report so we know what the winds are doing, because that's a big influence on the fire, and if for some reason it blows up and crosses our line, we usually have a contingency plan. We have several goals: one is, make sure everyone is safe and no one gets hurt; the other is to protect structures; our third would be containment – keeping the fire a certain size. An IC will always have three or four contingency plans so if it burns across a road and we can't hold it, then we go to the next road, and so on.

A good day is when the fire doesn't cross your line because you put in all that hard work. Depending on how thick the trees are, you can put in 100 yards a day because you are cutting and digging so much and if a fire jumps over that, you've just wasted a whole day. A perfect example was this year in Alaska. We put in a line for three days and then all of a sudden the wind and the humidity just lined up perfectly and conspired to cruise straight over our line. We had three helicopters trying to knock it down and it still jumped over. And we were right in what we call the 'hotline' where the fire's burning right next to you as you're cutting down trees and we still couldn't catch it. The next day, the conditions were better and we put another line around it. But it is annoying when you have put three or four days work in and you have to do it all over again. That'll be a bad day.

The fire is like a dragon. Or we'll call it the beast or something like that. When it's seriously gobbling, we'll say the area's been 'nuked', because it looks like a napalm drop. That doesn't happen that often. Maybe 10 per cent of the time. Pretty much everything would have to be perfect for it to start gobbling; it's just the craziest thing you've ever seen – this huge column of smoke and you can hear it from miles away, roaring. It sounds like a beast; like an animal. And you'll see 200–300-foot flame lengths. This thing will be just cruising or cranking through the woods. It's pretty intense to see. The other 90 per cent of the time, it's 2–3 feet high, just creeping around in the woods and every now and again a tree will catch fire. But when it's really gobbling, you pretty much get out of the way, there's nothing you can do.

I remember last year, we got a bunch of smoke up in the valley in Montana where I was working and we Google Earthed it and there was this fire of like 3,000–4,000 acres up in Canada and we just let it burn. That was ripping across Alberta. Pretty cool.

One of the biggest reasons everyone does it is because it's really fun and exciting. When you are out in the woods, in the wilderness, it is hard work, but rewarding. And you are helping people. A lot of the time we will save homes and we'll get some homeowners out, and just to see the look on their faces – how happy they are and how grateful – it's pretty rewarding. And you can make good money in a short amount of time – working hard and then getting time off. It's pretty exciting.

It's one of those jobs where you get a call and you get excited about it. If a fire blows up and goes crazy, most of the guys think it's pretty cool. We don't really want any rain because we want to keep working, and let's be honest, most of the guys are born pyromaniacs – they like to watch fire! It's pretty neat.

STORY TOLD BY DAVE

THE HOTSHOT (WILDLAND FIREFIGHTER)

 **DANGER FACT:**

During the 1949 Mann Gulch fire in Montana, 12 smokejumpers died when they lost their communication links, became disorientated, and were overtaken by the fire. In the 2009 Australian bushfires, at least 173 people died and over 2,029 homes and 3,500 structures were lost when they became engulfed by wildfire.

 **EXTREME FACT:**

Since 1965 Dave's 'Flathead Hotshot' crew have been on 406 fires for 2,319 days.

THE ICE ROAD TRUCKER

Extreme rating: ☠☠☠☠☠
Danger level: ▁▁▄▄■■■□□□
Criteria: Truck driving skills; winter driving skills; commercial Canadian driver's licence and one week on the ice-road driving programme
Skills: Determination; courage; confidence; stamina; problem solving; ability to work alone
Salary: US $40,000 (£25,000) in three months

When I was at school I had to do a report on something I didn't know anything about and I picked dirt bikes. I then took mechanics' classes, really liking engines and the way they work and then started racing motocross. I got a job delivering pizza and I really enjoyed being out of the building, getting in my car and driving around town, seeing what was going on. And I'm like, I really like this! It just kind of fit. It made sense to me. I had a goal – to be in a career by the age of 23 – and I decided to go for trucks because they were big, have engines, and I like them. I love being up high. And I love monster trucks and working trucks and bikes – anything with an engine.

So I started driving a school bus to get licensed and then went around and applied for jobs. Everywhere I went, I said, 'I'm going to drive a big truck someday. Are you willing to train me?' And if they said no, I didn't apply, and if they said yes, I did. Finally Carlile gave me the chance and I was in a small truck for a while, but when I finished my run every day, on my off time, I got into a big truck and drove around the yard getting used to shifting gears and backing trailers. That was the first time I'd ever been in a big truck. I started slowly working my way up. They licensed me about a year and a half later.

I had definitely made up my mind that trucking was what I wanted to do. I didn't want a normal job, like a nine-to-five. I didn't want to be in an office. I wanted to do a job that needed me to be outside and work physically so I wouldn't get flabby and big. I should have looked closer at truck drivers before I decided that! It was a way to be outside yet inside; you're in the truck and you're out travelling and you're getting paid to do it. And it's so fun. I'm glad I picked it, because I get to go to work in my pyjamas, I can listen to music all day long, and I have the best view, better than anybody's office.

I'm very creative and imaginative, and trucking kind of is. You wouldn't think it was that creative but when you're out in the middle of nowhere, you don't have phone service and something breaks, you have to be creative and logical to first find out what's wrong, then get your tools and see what you have to work with and then work out how you're going to fix it to get to where you're going. I've filled up the radiator with swamp water a few times just to make it. You use all kinds of different detachments and you get creative; like how to move fuel from one tank to another. It's fun.

If you feel like being social, you turn your radio on, and if you don't feel like being social, you turn it off. It's my social life and my private time. I guess not that many females do it. I don't necessarily understand why. But I really, really enjoy it. Maybe most think of it more as a 'male job', or boring, and go for something more exciting.

All the time I'm driving, I'm constantly having to think; it's not just about holding a steering wheel and shifting gears. You're thinking, 'OK, I'm about to pull this hill and I'm going to pull it in this gear. So how am

I going to get there? What percentage is the gradient? Am I going to do gear and a half or just half gears or full gears? Do I need to pre-cool the engine so I don't run out of RPM at the top?' It's the thinking that makes it so much fun.

And I love the freedom. I get to see bears, musk ox, caribou, moose, foxes, wolves, birds and other things that I never knew existed. I've seen two new animals in the last three years that I've never seen in my 25 years of living here. There's always something new to be discovered.

I've got a music playlist that matches parts of the road and that means something to where I am. It enhances the beauty. There's nothing like driving along at two o'clock in the morning and getting your own personal Northern Lights show that no one else in the world is seeing except you. My favourite tracks are 'Xpander' by DJ Sasha – I'm a techno person – and 'Heaven' by Moby or anything by Enya or Enigma.

We have two different radios. One is a short-range, CB radio, the other's long range which we use to talk to each other most of the time. We're usually on different channels, so we have the CB on one channel to know where each other's at on the road, and then the other to chit-chat and socialise, and get news and information; if the road's blocked or closed, someone's broken down, if there are storms coming…

The last few times I've run with my co-worker Rick who's got the same run as me. We talk all the way up to Prudhoe [Alaska] and keep each other awake in the middle of the night, then I run back with a couple friends of mine, we go on a different channel and chit-chat all the way back.

I have a truck that's assigned to me and I've had it for three years now, going on four. Heck, I've been married to this truck as long as my husband! Everything I own is in there and it stays there waiting for me to come trucking again. Its name is Wocket from Dr Seuss. It's my Wocket, and we talk to each other. I have a new top-of-the-line, amazing mattress. I've never wanted to climb into bed so bad as when I'm out trucking. I'll go trucking just to go to bed! I have an electric blanket in there too. It's behind the cab. The front of the truck is where I work and the back of the truck is where I live. So you take your shoes off before you come into my house. I don't have a kitchen, I just have a fridge; it's pretty much roughin' it; like camping. I have to pack stuff that's refrigerated and doesn't need to be heated. So a lot of peanut butter and jelly sandwiches, fruit and stuff that I can munch on. It's not the healthiest ever, but you've gotta take stuff that doesn't need blenders, frying pans or hot water.

I have the full winter gear: toe warmers, warm socks, snow trousers, hat and gloves and in those extreme temperatures, you get cold fast. I just jump back in the truck and warm up before I get out again. And I've got the electric blanket just in case I'm dying out there and if the truck ain't running, I can wrap up in that. Getting wet's the worst because it's really hard to get dry, especially if you don't have a source of heat.

We're all like a family out there. And it doesn't matter how you feel about someone, if they need help, you stop and help them. Your differences go aside when it comes to someone's life. There's been a few times that I've been stranded for a while. Like a storm comes in, the truck's stuck in a drift and I can't get out until the storm stops because no one can plough me out and I'm afraid of running out of fuel. I haven't, but you know, it's potentially dangerous. There's been a few times that my truck hasn't started and I've been lucky someone's been with me, because it gets really cold, really fast, so they push started to get the truck going again.

There were a couple of situations in Bolivia when we were hauling cocoa leaves; it was a national thing that they didn't want Americans messing with. Riots started, there were hostages being held, they wanted their cocoa leaves back and we were just trying to get out of there. It could have been bad, but we got everybody out OK, nobody got hurt. So that was interesting.

So many landslides I can't even count! In India, Libya and Peru, there were times that I had tyres hanging over the edge, I'd walk out to take a look but hardly consider it out of the ordinary. There's been a few times where the road gave away, the truck fell and a driver's died. Once, about an hour later, while a guy was down there dead in the truck, I had to pass a vehicle on the same spot. It took me about fifteen minutes to get by this guy, because I didn't want to move over any more. That was scary, just thinking that someone just died there and I was in the same spot doing the same thing.

On the Haul Road where I work, it's usually: 'Who's the bravest/dumbest (or youngest) and feels like fighting the elements?' Because if you hear it's going to storm, but not too badly (you might have to chain up to get through) some of us younger drivers will go for it because we don't mind fighting storms. But the older, more seasoned truckers tend to just wait it out. Then, the next morning, it's bright and sunny and beautiful, it's been ploughed, and they can go right through and not have to waste all that time doing all the hard work to make it through. So it's kind of who you trust running with and who has the energy to do it. You're either one of them that has the energy, or you sit back, relax, eat a nice meal and get a good night's sleep.

If it's really storming bad… well, I'm a professional and a lot of it is about making good choices. Most of the time I try not to take too many chances, but if I'm by myself, or if I have someone with me and we're running hard, having a good time and I'm feeling adventurous, we'll go for it. We'll put on chains and plough through drifts, no big deal. I wouldn't do anything dangerous. I save that for my time off!

It's not competitive. We're all out here doing the same thing. You're going to see the same people every single day, so you don't try to make anyone mad because you're going to pass them the next day. It's like a family. I mean, sometimes you get along with some of them and sometimes you don't, but you get to know everyone's names, their trucks, and who they work for. And you just work together to help each other get to where you're going. Like the other day, one of my trucks broke down and I didn't have a flight out of there so I just hitched a ride with a completely different company back to Fairbanks. We work together. It's a strange family but it's a good one.

The *Ice Road Truckers* TV show tries to make it look really competitive and like I have something to prove, when in reality I've already done that. The guys already know who I am and what I do, and I do it on or off camera, it doesn't matter. If the cameras are on, I'll help someone. If they're not on, I'll help someone. So I try to stay consistent and keep on doing and keep on being. And then when the TV came… it's almost like I had to *re*-prove myself to the world.

At the same time that I'm one of the guys up there, they still know that I'm a lady and they try to watch their language around me and not tell dirty jokes. I'm like a little sister or a daughter to a lot of them. And yet I'm still one of the guys and can hold my own. It's kind of a delicate balance I imagine for some of them to figure out what I am. And some are like, 'I don't help her at all. She can take care of herself.' So it's like, OK, that's cool. And others are willing to help and watch their language around me, or whatever. And I'm cussing up like a sailor next to them!

We definitely do stuff to the truck to handle the cold, like chains and a winter front to help the engine retain heat – and you can put a diesel additive into your fuel so it doesn't gel up. But you definitely change your driving depending on the temperatures. When it's warm out on pavement in summer you can just cruise along normally. When it's dark, you slow down because you can't see the animals on the road. And when it gets colder, right about freezing point, then you really slow down because of the ice melting and rain. Then when it gets to about… I don't know, zero to 25 below, it's really good trucking. The tyres are warm, the road is cold. The truck sticks to the road really good. When it gets to 40–50 below, then you slow down because you don't want to hit your brakes too hard or anything too hard because things will break. If you hit your brakes hard, you could pop a valve and it's plastic and you lose all your air. You don't want to do brakes a whole lot and you want to be really careful with everything plastic on your truck or even metal. You don't want to pound on things too hard or hit bumps too hard, because you'll break something.

The hardest trucking is mostly when the wind is blowing snow across the road so you can't see. It's really windy; really cold. Your truck won't hold heat. You're crossing through snowdrifts. Sometimes you make it, sometimes you don't. And then in doing that and spraying snow up onto the engine, sometimes hoses or tubes clog up or stuff breaks on the underside. So it's hard visibility when the snow's blowing like that. You can't see where the edges of the road are and you can't see over your hood. Sometimes my cab will overheat and I have to get out and scrape the ice off the front so that my truck can breathe again.

I ended up falling in love with it and what keeps me doing it is being alone – I love being alone and thinking, processing and being creative, coming up with ideas. I love that. And listening to music and being in my pyjamas. And just being out in the middle of nowhere with no phone service or anything, watching the Northern Lights… it's so quiet out there that you can almost hear them. Then there's the stars… you can lay out there in the middle of nowhere surrounded by absolute wilderness. It's just… the beauty of it. When you're not simply enjoying the scenery, it's the challenge. You're learning constantly and I love to learn, I love to be challenged and then you feel proud of yourself because you just overcame something amazing. You got the job done, or you went above and beyond. It fulfils so many things: my alone time, my accomplishments, my creativity. And then just being partnered up with an amazing machine like that. You know, I don't work without it and it don't work without me.

THE ICE ROAD TRUCKER

On TV I want to show that people – anybody – can live their dreams and they can come true if you make the sacrifices that you need to. What I'm hopefully portraying to people is how much fun life is if you let it be. I want everyone to experience life the way that I do. It's so much fun.

STORY TOLD BY LISA

An ice road consists of 87 per cent ice and a lot of trucks have fallen through because even where the ice freezes several feet thick the roads can only support so much weight. Dangers on the Dalton Road (the 'Haul Road') include icy roads (the surface is 2-inch-thick ice over gravel or whatever is underneath) steep hills, hairpin turns, narrow roads, avalanches, white-outs and travelling over frozen sea ice in −70°F (−21°C).

A spin-off of the *Ice Road Truckers* programme – *Deadliest Roads* – covers 'The Yungas (Death) Road' in Bolivia where the death rate has been estimated at 200–300 per year.

The first season of *Ice Road Truckers* featured a 370-mile-long ice road in Canada, supplying Yellowknife and three diamond mines. Truckers are not allowed to travel the winter road alone, so three trucks are dispatched from Yellowknife about every 20 minutes. Ice trucking requires average speeds of 20 miles per hour.

Lisa covers the Dalton Highway ice road in Alaska which is 414 miles long, with up to a 12 per cent gradient. It's one of the most isolated roads in the US with just three towns along the route.

THE ICELANDIC
FISHERMAN

My father was a lighthouse keeper and as a boy I would go up with him to the top and watch the boats. It was fascinating in good weather, just as it was unbearable to watch in bad weather when they were in danger.

I have been fishing off Iceland now for 30 years with my son Petur Petursson the sixth and my brother. Running the boat is a tough job even for three able men, as we work a lot if we fish a lot. We need to be physically fit, strong and healthy – both body and soul.

It sometimes bothers me that I only have family members in my crew, especially when we are heading out in dicey or critical weather; half the family would be gone if my son and I go under. Weather changes so quickly here in Iceland that it's difficult to predict exactly when the storms will hit and how hard they will hit. We're very open to the weather systems of the North Atlantic Ocean.

In the beginning of my career we had to rely completely on the weather forecast on the radio, which would only be broadcast a few times a day. We learned to read the signs and patterns for weather changes, combine that with the forecast and then interpret what that would mean for us. A great deal more boats went under in those years than do now. You learn from experience, add the information and get guidance from your intuition. If you have your nets in where the weather is forecast to become worse, you bring them in and move to a safer area while the weather passes through. It can be terribly cold working outdoors in the North Atlantic winter.

What helps is that weather forecasting has improved in the last few years. We get more accurate forecasts and the forecast computer programs are very good – at least for weather conditions expected in the next 24 hours, although we have to take the long-term forecast into consideration when putting down the nets, so that we'll be able to get them back up before a storm hits.

We also have a support system through the other boats. We all help and support each other. Since my boat is relatively small and I fish closer to land, I can call up the captains on the bigger boats to ask what the weather is like out where they are. We can see all the ships on the computer – this has become so visual – so when we are wondering whether to go out or not I call the bigger boats and they give us information, which helps. I think that the same applies in other situations. The more information you have, the better decisions you can make.

For the smaller boats the biggest danger is the ocean itself. If we hit difficulty it's important to avoid making mistakes which so often cause accidents to happen and can be costly. It's also important to keep the boat in peak condition, so that limits the danger of breakdown at sea.

I was seasick when I started – and it took me a month to get over it. The best thing is that on a good day, you forget how you suffered on the bad days. Then you just enjoy life. I think it's a great human quality that we tend to forget bad experiences very quickly.

We go out a lot. We fish for cod from December to the end of April – during this period we go out every day if weather permits. During the summer, May to November, we fish for monkfish – then we go out four days a week, as we leave the nets in for longer.

We have all types of persons in this profession. You need to work hard at what you are doing to be well above average. The same law applies to everything. Those who are successful are usually the ones who have put more effort into their job. Some men are of course clever and some are lucky – and get ahead that way – but most of the time it depends on how much effort you put in.

I have been called the King of Arnarstapi harbour because I am a hard worker – so success has followed that. We are highly motivated by our work, competitive and want to do well. I started with nothing when I bought my first boat, so there were only two options; either do well, or give up, and I prefer the former.

Foul weather for a long period of time is the most difficult part of the profession. Having to wait or go out in it every day is very tiring and nerve-racking. This is when the weather is so bad that you *can* go, but only just. The saying here in Iceland is that when you lose your nerve to go out in weather like this, then you might just as well quit because then you have lost what is needed.

When we are fishing a lot and get long periods of this type of weather it is very trying for all of us. The boat moves so much, it requires great physical effort just to stand and work in weather like this for 8–10 hours a day. It is really hard labour and after a tour in this weather we are physically much more tired; then we may go out in good weather and catch perhaps 20 tonnes… and you are not tired at all.

There are no two days the same at sea. The conditions, the weather, the fishing grounds, everything changes all the time. One day you may be surrounded by thousands of seabirds, the next there may be hundreds of whales, anything from humpbacks to small minke whales – these ever-changing surroundings. We often set out in darkness and then when the first light of day appears and the rays of the sun start illuminating everything – and the sun's light reflects differently out at sea than it does ashore – we witness something amazing.

Seeing the whales is indescribable. We have had humpbacks surface so close to the boat that when we were pulling in the buoy, they were touching it. To see them come up when you are pulling in the net, with water and capelin flowing out of their mouths as they surface and dive again – I think this is the most amazing sight I have seen. The humpbacks can eat such a huge amount; up to a tonne in their mouth at one time. It's incredible to see them work together. They drive the capelin into a large cluster and then a few whales surface from the centre of the shoal – and the capelin and the ocean water flows out of their mouth, running down the sides, while they filter the food from the water.

Killer whales are a detrimental animal, I must say [swears]. They're brutes. They work together and kill both the small and larger whales. They are not like the orcas we see in Sea World; in nature they live up to their name.

It's always great to hit good weather, calm seas and a lot of fishing on the same day. Catching a big flounder [halibut] is always memorable. We can get them as big as 220–330 pounds. There is a huge difference in seeing a halibut come out of the sea, compared to seeing a 45-pound salmon come out of the river. We catch the flounder on a line with hooks, so you are always in for a surprise when you bring in the line. I really enjoy fishing for them.

A good day is when I fish a lot, when the weather is good – although I must say that the season I love most is spring, when the sun starts warming your back as you work.

STORY TOLD BY PETUR

DANGER FACT:

Commercial fishing is still considered to be the most dangerous occupation in the world, with an annual fatality rate of 116 deaths per 100,000. According to Petur, 'We have never had an army in Iceland or been at war with anyone other than the elements and the sea – and sometimes people over our fishing limits!'

EXTREME FACT:

Fishermen endure storms, fog, wind and hazardous working conditions, which constantly put them at risk. Around the British Isles – up to the 'Southeast Iceland' sea area – the Shipping Forecast broadcasts weather warnings four times a day via the Met Office and the BBC. An 'imminent gale' means that a gale is expected within six hours, 'expected soon' is within six to twelve hours and 'later' means in more than twelve hours' time. The distinctive sound of the Shipping Forecast has become an enduring part of the BBC Radio schedule and is listened to by many more than those who rely on the information for their safety.

THE INTERNATIONAL
SEARCH AND RESCUE
OFFICER

Extreme rating: ☠☠☠☠☠
Danger level: ▬▬▪▪▪▪▪▢▢▢▢
Criteria: Ideally search, rescue or related experience such as firefighting, paramedic, humanitarian aid, flood rescue; be available at short notice
Skills: Team player; strong work ethic for long hours in physically tough conditions; ability to cope with the duress and hazards; empathy with the local affected population; resourceful; adaptable; problem solving
Salary: Paid leave from another profession, e.g. firefighter, RNLI, paramedic

I belong to the International Search and Rescue (ISAR) Team which is part of the official response to earthquakes and disasters overseas. The team is sent out by DFID, the Department for International Development, under the UK banner. After 9/11, the UK reviewed its resilience and started a £200-million (US $311-million) programme called 'New Dimension', which reviewed urban search and rescue, CBRN (chemical, biological, radiological and nuclear) and major flooding. As part of that,

I was one of the initial people chosen to go out to Texas and train with American urban search and rescue (USAR) teams.

My first RNLI flood rescue deployment was the year of the tsunami, in February 2005, to Guyana in South America. We flew into Suriname, drove over the border and spent two to three weeks working on the Mahaica River, doing flood reconnaissance work for NGOs (non-governmental organisations) and certain aid agencies in Guyana for the affected population.

A flood is a terribly messy disaster because it wipes through but then leaves stagnant water, mixes up all the dust and debris and turns it into a slurry. So I suppose in terms of mess, you could say a flood is equally, if not more devastating, than an earthquake. I think people underestimate floods. The other thing with a flood is, if you take a high street and put it under 10 feet of water and leave that for a couple of days, the hazards are significant. If you're walking along and a manhole cover's been lifted up by the flood, there's potentially a hidden 20-foot drop there. There's street furniture you might get your foot stuck in, the current picks up, and then you're trapped. A flood creates unseen hazards.

In Guyana, we were using our flood rescue skills and working in a non-standard hazardous environment. When you deploy overseas, you have to be completely self-contained. That is, you mustn't be a drain on the resources of the country because they've got enough problems. So you deploy as a complete, self-contained unit with food, water, fuel, resources and then get on with it. Often there's no running water, no power. Wherever you turn up is where you have to live and work.

We set up a base of operations (BOO) and that becomes our focal point. From there, we push out into the field and come back to base each day. If there's a building that we can utilise, we will. If not, we take tents and resources, so we just need a space. We've set up in football stadiums, jungles, hotel lobbies. It can literally be anywhere.

Guyana's quite an interesting place and as it's a developing country, safety and security are legitimate issues that have to be continually managed. But more importantly, we still have to undertake our role. So, we always consider where we are, assess the risk, and agree control measures. Particularly in Guyana, there were certain places we couldn't go to and we had a night-time curfew, so after dark it was back to base. In Georgetown – the main capital – there were shootings most evenings, which was the normal pattern of life, that's typical for some environments we go to and you have to expect that. More and more, you have to factor it in; it'd be irresponsible if you didn't.

In 2009, I deployed to Indonesia, western Sumatra. There was a large earthquake and a significant international response. We deployed on behalf of the UK government to Padang under the direction of a United Nations UNDAC team (United Nations Disaster Assessment Coordination). We set up a base of operations with the other international rescue teams. The idea is that the UN coordinates all the international teams, so the right teams, equipment and resources are delivered and directed and the operations are as efficient as possible, supporting and working with the local and national authorities, which is paramount. It's the lynchpin of what we do.

When you first get to an earthquake, a flood, or a disaster, it's normally chaos. So there is a level of confusion, but we operate using international guidelines and everyone knows the framework. Once you put that framework together, no matter how bad it is, the response starts to take structure. Initially you slow down the decline, hopefully get it to a steady state, and then start implementing. Everyone follows international guidelines; that's common standard.

If you take an earthquake as an example, the immediate first days will be search and rescue; that's paramount, but it's only a relatively short window of operation. International Search and Rescue Teams are UN-certified as heavy, medium or light teams. A heavy rescue team has 60–70 people, specialist equipment, medics and search dogs. As you go down the scale, medium and light are just reductions on the equipment cache and the numbers of people, and light can move more rapidly. This is a global standard, so if we're working with any other countries, we know each other's capability because we're rated under the same UN system.

So the first period of any disaster is the search and rescue phase. It's obviously organised but is also a blitz mentality. You've got to get in there because the survival window is extremely limited depending on where you are. Interestingly, when we went to Haiti last year, because it wasn't the rainy season and because the type of construction was relatively inexpensive – concrete roof, concrete floor, two concrete walls – the construction fell over but there were voids left by the lean-to set-up. These voids were very cool and dry because of the season, so the survivability window was considerably longer. This means that the search and rescue phase in Haiti was pushed back days and days – it was probably one of the most successful search and rescue missions ever.

Once that phase finishes, or starts to draw to an end, you then move on to the humanitarian phases. The humanitarian stage is based on providing aid in clusters, so shelter might be a cluster. I've just come back from Turkey and the Turkish authorities requested international assistance for shelter and shelter only. They didn't need any other resources because they had it well covered. They needed shelter because they had about 25,000 people displaced where their homes and habitats had been destroyed. It was in the highest part of Turkey, 6,560 feet plus, winter was fast approaching and they needed to set up shelter for IDPs, which is internally displaced persons. So that's an example of a cluster. You get a food cluster, medical cluster, sanitation, education. So the job you have depends on where you fit into that scheme of things.

I'm also trained in coordination and assessment for the EUCPT (European Union Civil Protection Team), where we go in at the rapid onset of a disaster, and coordinate and assess the situation and needs at the request of the affected country, working in support with the UNDAC teams.

My role in Haiti was rapid assessment; that meant going out every day to assess the needs of the affected population in terms of search and rescue, humanitarian requirements: food, shelter, medical, etc. I would go out, build information, and bring that back to base. That information is then correlated and pushed out to the wider humanitarian family. So the importance of getting that information is critical. We try to avoid duplication and match the need to the response. Lots of people and countries want to donate aid, equipment and resources but it's important that the right equipment and resources are donated and delivered. If you get too much of one thing, it denies another area and it clogs up the infrastructure, so it's important that the information you give back is succinct and accurate.

In Haiti, we went out by vehicle a lot of the time to undertake needs assessments. It's important to get boots on the ground and build up a relationship with the affected population. You have to be very focused on what you're doing. You can't offer any direct assistance at this stage. You have to go in, explain what you're doing and get the critical information back, so the right resources can be deployed as effectively as possible. Haiti was quite extreme because it was a massive earthquake in a very underdeveloped country. It had a United Nations stabilisation force there already, which was the critical infrastructure managing the country day to day, and when the earthquake struck, it also struck that critical function, so it had a double impact. It was an extreme situation.

We were working with UN staff in-country and after a couple of days you could see how it affected them, because they'd lost both local and international staff in the earthquake. It was something that we were well aware of. It was difficult, but everyone was together; it was very much a global family working within a local village.

Haiti was also an interesting place because the security situation was demanding and required a higher level of control measures than a lot of other countries we go to. So everywhere we went, we required clearance and an armed escort, whether it was military or UN police.

When you go to countries, you need to look at their normal pattern of life. In Guyana, looting most evenings was normal. In Haiti, there might be shootings in the evenings and looting. But that's the normal pattern of life. That's what happens in certain countries; you have to accept that to some extent. It's important not to put yourself at risk, so you do a security plan and it's essential that you follow that plan, but it's equally important that you still carry out your job to the best of your abilities. Haiti was easy to some extent, because there was absolutely nothing there; there was complete and utter devastation. So we could carry out our role in absolute entirety.

We did a lot of assessments in Haiti where we were not only going out day to day in ground vehicles but also conducting aerial assessments in civilian chartered helicopters or military aircraft such as the American Black Hawks. The Black Hawks supplied a security arrangement as well. They have incredible flying capability so when we liaise with the aircrew, we are able to detail our flight plan more. They are able to fly us in and we can pinpoint exactly where we want to drop; for instance, football stadiums or car parks in the city areas. They drop us down; we get off with a discreet security detail, go out, do our assessment and then call the helicopter back to take us away.

A helicopter's like a people magnet, it draws people in. Once the helicopter is gone, the situation eases and we can go and find the local mayor or the local village officials.

When you're in-country, on a mission, you have to be very empathetic – that's key. That's why you need to meet with the people, shake their hands, touch them, sit down with them and get onto their level. When I was in Turkey we went up to one of the villages in the outer-lying area to speak to a family who had lost their daughter and granddaughter in the earthquake. You're in there speaking to them one day, then the next, speaking to the governor of the province. That's part of the job. That's what makes the role so dynamic, but very humbling.

In Haiti one day we were doing a vehicle assessment and part of the road gave way and the vehicle dropped into a hole. Within two or three minutes, we probably had a thousand people surrounding us. My colleague and I looked at each other and thought, 'Well, this can go one of two ways.' We then just asked the local population: 'Could you lift us up?' and they physically lifted the Land Cruiser out of the hole, put it back onto the roadway and we drove off! It's one of those odd moments.

In Haiti, I never felt in true danger. We were deployed to Léogâne which was one of the worst affected areas and we were the first Western assessors in there, the first responders. That was a couple of days after the earthquake. There was a sense of awe and shock. We subsequently went back, 24 and 48 hours afterwards, and the second and third time, there was a change in the pattern of life. We were still trying to push resources in and the shock had turned into, 'Why aren't we being helped?' You could sense the tension in the atmosphere. Very quickly we were able to get resources in there: water, food, hospitals, etc. You can measure that mood and get a feel for it.

You have to be very careful. I'm fortunate in that I've got an urban search and rescue background, so I'm familiar with structural collapse. With assessment missions, it's important that you bring your own skills to bear as well as those you train for, but you do have to be very, very careful. When you have the initial earthquake, you get aftershocks; buildings become unsafe and there are numerous injuries from secondary collapse. A building suffers major damage from an earthquake, and it's got elements of structure that might fall or drop off. The other thing is, in hot or cold countries regardless, the time of day matters. Buildings heat up at different rates. So early morning and late at night, the temperature can affect the structure; you need to be careful with that and also general debris. We had numerous vehicle punctures in Haiti. By not checking your vehicle, not having a jack and a couple of spare tyres… You're completely knackered, so it's important to get the basics right. Driving is one of the most dangerous things we do.

There are procedures that we adopt where we will make a structure safe. We can put in timber or metal shores which secure it as we go in because obviously it's essential that we don't have any further casualties.

Search dogs are fantastic. The importance of their role shouldn't be underestimated. If you imagine you've got someone trapped in a large, five-storey hotel or housing block, to physically search for that person you need to target an area where they are, because when you start having to break concrete and break into the building, it takes a massive amount of resources, equipment and time. If you drill through 18 inches of concrete and put the hole in the wrong place because you're in the wrong void, it can be disastrous. We use audio and acoustic listening devices and search equipment, but the benefit of a dog is that you can put it onto a rubble pile or a collapsed structure and it will give an early indication of the scent and therefore an area to target; we then try and back that up with an electronic device.

Causalities radiate a scent. The scent normally drifts off in a cone and drifts out of the building. The skill of the search dogs is incredible. They can track down that scent and indicate to a much smaller area working back to the source of the scent or as close as physically possible. Search and rescue dogs can also indicate that it's a live casualty, which is important. They're predominantly Border collies and spaniels, but there are other breeds used by the UK and other countries. The dogs are a part of the team; an essential part.

An element of the job is hostile environment working. So you do your job, but come back to base for your personal administration and hygiene, which are critical. If you come down with food poisoning, pick up a bug, don't clean your water or dehydrate, you're going to become a liability and a risk to your other team members. So that's an important part of what we do. We maintain inoculations. We don't share water, we check the source. We follow basic hygiene rules. But what I tend to find, when I work in those environments, I follow health and safety rules more closely because I can see what actually happens if I don't.

We were in Haiti for two weeks or thereabouts; working 18–20-hour days for the first week in 40°C of heat, on rations, living in tents. For the first four or five days there was no sanitation: no running water, no hot showers. The team bond, the team dynamic, is crucial. You have to have a certain mentality, understanding and black humour – humour of the darkest kind. It's normal and natural and healthy. You tend to find that people who can't work in that environment tend not to stay very long. But the training identifies that, so by the time you go you feel you've got a steady team. You do experience low points as well as highs, but that's life.

Most of us who do the international work volunteer to do it as part of normal duty, for instance I'm a fire officer in my day job and crew for my local RNLI. Whatever role or rank you do in the service, you take on additional duties, but you're not paid extra. It's just part of the job. It's a vocation. People that join tend to stay. I invariably bump into colleagues I know on deployment in missions from other countries; it's a very local family.

Wherever I've gone, we've always made a difference. When you're on the ground you can see the difference. I think that's important. Because if you're one to one with someone, you demonstrate you care. You've come all the way from this country to their country to help and assist. It shows empathy, it shows concern. And that may have a long-term effect. We have a set of skills and training that allows us to do something in situations where we can make a difference. That's what drives me.

STORY TOLD BY JOHN

In the 12 days following the 2010 Haiti quake, at least 52 aftershocks measuring 4.5 or greater were recorded. The Haitian government reported that an estimated 316,000 people died, 300,000 were injured and 1,000,000 made homeless. Following the 2011 Tōhoku earthquake the Japanese National Police Agency confirmed 15,845 deaths, 5,893 injured and 3,380 people missing.

The magnitude of the 2011 Japan earthquake was one of the highest recorded in the last century, measuring 9.0 on the Richter scale. Only three were greater: Sumatra, Alaska and Valdivia in Chile. Haiti measured 7.0. It is estimated that around 500,000 earthquakes occur each year, about 100,000 of which can be felt.

THE LIFEBOAT COXSWAIN

Extreme rating: ☠☠☠☠☠
Danger level: ▁▁▄▄■■■■□□□
Criteria: Over 17 years old (with parents' permission) or over 18 and under 45 (inshore lifeboat) or 55 (all-weather lifeboat); pass a medical and eyesight test; be physically fit; live and/or work close to a lifeboat station; ideally have some relevant experience being at sea, conducting rescues or first aid
To be a coxswain: Must undertake all crew qualifications; training to standard of Commercial skipper for operations up to 60 nautical miles offshore; demonstrate competence against the RNLI Operational Training Standards for Coxswains; separate assessment by RNLI inspector
Skills: Be a team player and accepted by the rest of the crew; enjoy hard physical work; get on well with other people; communicate easily; obey orders when required to
Salary: From £23,740 (US $36,970)

Within the port of Harwich there is Felixstowe, which is the largest container port in the UK. At Harwich International Port, we have a cruise terminal for cruise ships and passengers from Denmark or Holland and a lot of roll-on, roll-off ships. So within the Harwich area, over the course of the year, an average of one ship moves every 12 minutes. On top of that, there is a fishing community, leisure-based marinas, jet skis and surfboarders. We deal with everything from the very deep-water ships – the 'ultra large' ships – to kids on lilos or dinghies playing near the beach. We encompass it all. We are one of the busier RNLI (Royal National Lifeboat Institution) stations, with over 100 services a year, some of which stretch across to Hook of Holland and Zeebrugge for 80–90 miles. That route obviously takes a lot of time and, in bad weather, a lot of effort. The North Sea is a dangerous place in the wrong weather.

My rescue average is almost 30 a year for nearly 30 years – about 1,000 rescues, both inshore and offshore, here and at other stations. So, one or two!

I am one of the relatively few paid RNLI lifeboat crew members – at some of the busiest stations, full-time coxswains and mechanics are in paid positions – but 95 per cent of the charity's lifeboat crew members around the coasts of the UK and Ireland are volunteers. They carry a pager and are on-call, ready and willing to drop whatever they're doing when the emergency call comes in, to go and launch the lifeboat to save people at sea.

I live within 1.5 miles of the station, and apart from my two weekends off a month, I am on call 24 hours a day, seven days a week. I'm not far away from hanging up the pager, but I will believe in the lifeboat service forever. Without question. If you didn't believe in it, I don't think you'd be able to do it. It's belief in the institution, the service and belief in the crews that has carried me through for 30 years as a volunteer and a full-timer. If the crew don't turn up, I don't go anywhere; the crew are far, far more important than I am. I'm just one; they are the whole team and I'm an extremely lucky coxswain because I have a very marine-wise crew, many of whom work the sea for their profession.

We have the largest of the RNLI boats; the Severn class, which can take six crew and achieve a speed of 25 knots. In fact, Harwich was the first station to take a Severn class and she still remains with us. We also have an Atlantic 75 inshore lifeboat, due to be upgraded soon to an Atlantic 85.

THE LIFEBOAT COXWAIN

The North Sea in an easterly or north-easterly gale can be an extremely rough and very difficult working environment. One of our services a couple of years ago took 23 hours from start to finish in gale force 9, gusting 10. Services can change. If it's a search it will run on as long as physically possible or until conditions and daylight mean it has to be terminated. Once we're there, we generally stay.

On board, going out on a shout, the noise level is extremely high: radios are chattering, the hull bangs as you crash from one wave to the next and the engines are very noisy. It's a loud and violent environment to be in. You get thrown from side to side, you pitch up and down. The sea can be very confused here. There's no definite wave pattern. All of the seats have harnesses, so when weather conditions get bad, the crew strap down.

The worst I've seen… well, the hurricane of 1987 wasn't very good. At its peak, at 100 knots plus, the Harwich lifeboat was launched on a service to a ship called the *Silver Falcon*. The conditions that day were extremely difficult. The waves get knocked down by the strong winds but spume rises above the water and so visibility reduces. In hurricane-force winds, it's sheer violence in everything around you.

As conditions deteriorate, some rescues become more and more difficult for many different reasons. You may launch for what you think is going to be a relatively simple job, but by the time you arrive, many other factors come in to play; the location may not have been correct, or maybe the casualties are unable to help themselves due to injury or seasickness; so rescues often become far more difficult than you first thought. You can't have an exact game plan. Things can change very quickly. Your best-laid plans may have to suddenly readjust because of what you find once you arrive.

Of course you have to demonstrate leadership skills. You have to ensure that, on certain jobs, you're picking the right mix of people, whether it's the guy who's a sailor and can deal with the yacht, whether it's the guy who's a paramedic for the medical job… That's where leadership starts:

when the crew first turn up at the station. From there, you hope that you give confidence to the crew for whatever the job may be. And even when you're thinking, 'Bloody hell, this is getting tight,' if you can hold the confident attitude, the crew pick up on that. They relate to the vibes you're giving off. Also you get to know their other halves, their children. So you have a responsibility to make sure that you bring those guys and girls back safely, back to their families, along with whoever you go out for. These are my personal beliefs. They've carried me through so far and not only do my crew appear to have total trust in me, I have total trust in them. It's a two-way street.

The worst job I've ever been on was a friend of my son's who, along with several other boys, were wave jumping on a promenade. He was unfortunately swept away, to his death. And along with two other crew, Scott and Glen, recovering him and then airlifting him to a helicopter was an extremely, extremely difficult personal moment for me. That is my worst. Any rescues that involve children and loss of life – none are good. Nobody could have done any more, but we were beaten by conditions and the weather; it wasn't successful and therefore it remains my worst memory. Any that are non-successful are bad. I would love to say that I've had a whole career and never lost any, but it doesn't work that way. You never win this battle with the elements. We try and hold our own, but we never actually beat it. They're all bad memories when you have a loss of life.

We once had a report of a light aircraft pitching into the sea. Not very funny at first, at all. We launched and got to the search area, where we were informed by a yacht that he'd picked up a swimmer who he thought had been drinking because he claimed he was from a plane. Sure enough it was the pilot, totally unmarked, totally undamaged, swimming along. He'd been doing aerobatics and got too low. You think: he's just come out of the sky, his plane has sunk and the people who pick him up won't even believe where he's from! There are amusing moments, but that's good; crews need to have a laugh to balance the downside.

Another one which wasn't funny at the time was where we were doing a transfer of an RNLI crew member to a yacht in rather poor weather and we asked them to drop their sails but they couldn't. So we pulled up alongside, my crew member moved forwards, went to make the leap across to the casualty vessel and the yacht's sail came round, whipped him off our deck, wrapped him up and deposited him on the casualty vessel. That was the only time we've ever achieved a transfer in that manner!

We do get people who come back and say thank you. In fact, yesterday a Christmas box arrived from a gentleman who had had a major heart attack on board. He was worked on by the Harwich crews for a considerable amount of time and will quote to everybody in his local village that he's here because we were there. It's extremely heart-warming when these people do come back.

We are there for anybody, but others are there for me. It's the belief that if you are in difficulty, somebody else will come and get you. It's the fourth emergency service. An amazing organisation, staffed by many volunteers who, I have to say, are the real heroes for me. Those that give up time with their families, their time at work, and still go out there and do this amazing job.

We go out at night for probably 35–40 per cent of the time. I think the reason is that people will try to battle on during the day, but as darkness descends on them, it brings added fear to whatever their problem is. Darkness compounds it; things look worse at night, you can't read the wave patterns so well. So quite a high percentage of our jobs are done at night. That, of course, makes our life more difficult. I'd rather go and get them in daytime and I'm sure my crew would too. But we go with what we get. One or two o'clock is a tough time to get up and go. You leave your nice, warm bed and suddenly you're in an extremely cold and hostile North Sea.

To be honest, it's one of those jobs where things are good when we're not doing anything. Which is a strange job to have, but like many other emergency services, it's true. The quiet days are the good days. Whether we get them or not is in the lap of the gods.

STORY TOLD BY SMUDGE

In 1981 the Penlee lifeboat *Solomon Browne* was lost – with all eight crew – going to the aid of the freighter Union Star. Sixteen people died including eight volunteer lifeboat crew.

Following the *Marchioness* and *Bowbelle* collision on the Thames in 1989, where 51 lives were lost, the RNLI established its first stations on the Thames in 2001. Tower Lifeboat is now the busiest of all lifeboat stations (it rescued 148 people in 2009) and is crewed 24 hours a day, 365 days a year.

In 1881 silver medals were awarded for the saving of seven people from the wreck of the steamer *Ingerid*. The lifeboat had to break through ice to get out of the harbour and then crew rowed for over eight hours before reaching the wreck.

The RNLI has saved more than 139,000 lives since its foundation in the early 1820s. The year 2010 was the RNLI's second busiest in its history with 8,713 launches and 8,313 people rescued – the most reported in a single year so far.

THE RALLY DRIVER

Extreme rating: ☠☠☠☠☠

Danger level: ▁▃▅▆█████☐☐☐

Criteria: Driving licence; rally competition licence; rally car equipped with safety equipment; MSA (Motor Sports Association) logbook; navigator or co-driver; money or sponsorship

Skills: Intuitive driving skills; navigation; courage; quick reflexes; power-sliding; handbrake turns; mechanical skills

Salary: From nothing to millions of pounds! Some top names have allegedly earned £6 million (US $9.3 million) for a two-year deal, and €5 million (US $6.3 million) in another case

I got involved in off-road racing – rallying – when I was 17. I got hooked on it and worked in a garage to save up the money. I've rallied for ten years in this country and then decided to go racing in France – it's a bit faster over there. There are no restrictions in France, nothing you have to adhere to; not like the FIA regulations (Fédération Internationale de l'Automobile). You've got a blank sheet of paper so you can design and build cars that are more rally orientated; with a tubular framework, fibreglass body and any engine you like. They're then phenomenally fast and powerful. You can literally have any power you want. If you want a big 600-hp [horsepower] Chevrolet engine you can put that in and go racing. Drive through the forest as fast as you can. Sometimes that's not necessarily the best thing though. You actually want something relatively light and nimble.

I won the French championship with a car that looked like a Peugeot 206 World Rally Car but it was specialist built with a tubular framework, BMW mid engine and gearbox at the front. I did it with a farmer friend of mine who was my navigator! It's brilliant fun. Racing up the top of the mountains – like the Pyrenees – with sheer drops over the side.

The whole course is tricky; it's not like on a track or Brands Hatch. On your average French stage, which could be 5–7.5 miles, it'll be through mud, tyre tracks, woods, then maybe a fast straight when you are up to 120 miles per hour, then right down to walking pace round some bollards or hay bales, off out into a field… there's obstacles all the way. You can drive through forests at 100 miles per hour and there's trees every second whizzing past you while you're on a track just 8 feet wide. Then you have to go over a cattle grid and it narrows down to a gate width and you have to go over it at 80 miles per hour… It gets quite interesting!

There are some stages that are really precarious. Many of the stages in the south of France are in the Pyrenees with a big climb to the top. You have to wind your way up the side of the mountain, through the forest, and there are a lot of straights and fast bits before the next stage. That can get quite hairy. We've had some really dicey moments where, looking back on it, you think: 'That was close.' The co-driver wouldn't have said anything at the time, but when you are sideways round a corner at 70 miles per hour on loose gravel and the back wheel is scrabbling at the edge of a long drop… you wouldn't want to go down it. You would be in a pretty poor state. Maybe it didn't have quite as much grip as you thought, so you kick the power on – and then you've made it! Sometimes there's a look between you and the co-driver…

The older you get, the more you start to think about self-preservation. When you are younger you just don't think about it, it's just a track.

THE RALLY DRIVER

In the car there's a roll cage and we wear a helmet and fireproof overalls. We also have to wear a HANS [head and neck support] device now which goes over your neck to stop it from snapping or going into your chest. It tethers the neck, basically, which is a bit uncomfortable because in rallying you have to look out the side a lot; most of the time you are going sideways and you're always looking around. So if your neck is tethered you can't turn more than a certain degree; it's quite cumbersome and not very nice. I don't like them but they just take a while to get acclimatised to. That's it, there's no other padding.

I've turned the car over lots of times, you just get used to it. Landing on the roof or whatever, end over end a few times; you get a bit of neck pain afterwards, but nothing major. You just roll over and sit and wait in the car for spectators to put you upright again and then you drive off if it's not too battered!

Crowds can get in the way, which always makes you a bit nervous. It's better now. They used to be out on the edge of the corners on the apex, just standing in all the wrong places and you had to slow up a little bit.

You do need to be pumped up, but then you can't be too pumped up as it all goes a bit ragged. It's about being nice and smooth, although you've got to be quick and able to react. Sometimes you do a stage and you think, 'I'm really going to go for it now' – and you're hard on the car, really aggressive, really unsympathetic on the mechanical side of it.

Then over the years you learn to do it differently. You take a different line and drive more smoothly. Speed might look spectacular – wide and flooring it, rooster tails of mud and gravel flying everywhere and the crowd loving it, but then if you just dive neatly into the corner, quickly turn and go, you're probably quicker. It looks more spectacular the other way and you may *feel* like you're going faster but you're not. You learn a different approach with experience and years of doing it. You might try a different route or sometimes it comes by accident. I've had problems, such as the engine overheating where you are short-changing and trying to keep things going, and thought, 'I must have lost loads of time on that' – but then you look at your time and you're just eight seconds slower, which isn't as bad as you thought. So sometimes it can work out unintentionally.

It's about balancing wisdom and courage. You still need the courage when push comes to shove but it's a calculated courage. You have to calculate what's coming next and then be both wise and courageous in how you tackle it.

You need to set up a turn nicely. If you are going too fast the car won't have changed its attitude, it hasn't started to turn nicely, it will just plough through maybe a big burn of sand or stone which slows you down and then you have to recover from it. It should be nice and smooth and calm in the right gear. Sometimes if you've got it on full lock and you're slamming on the brakes, it won't turn unless you take your foot off the brake. It can be frightening. Sometimes I don't know why I do it!

The dangerous corners are the ones that you feel really good about. If you get them right, you think, *I know that nobody else would have gone round there that fast. I know I just got that absolutely perfect.* Other drivers would have erred on the side of caution because of the danger and gone a lot slower – because if they get it wrong, it's game over. If you do get a corner like that right, there's a real buzz. It's a great feeling being in control going sideways. You know that it was just absolutely perfect. You couldn't have gone any faster than that.

When I first started racing in France I would come up to the finish, look at the leader board and think, 'They're 40 seconds faster than me! Where did they get that time?!' It's just more practice, doing more of it, learning your trade, getting better and better and then the gap comes down to 25 seconds, and then 15, and the more you do it, you get within two seconds of the top guy and then, before you know it, you are the top guy! You've made it!

THE RALLY DRIVER

It's also about good teamwork; you get to know each other's style. Your co-driver needs to understand what information you need and when; what corner's coming up and what's after the corner. They have to be good at writing the notes and good at reading them out. You may lose time when your navigator is looking at the pace notes or if it's at the bottom of a page and they haven't turned over to see the next manoeuvre. They may call '100, 4, left' (i.e. in 100 metres, angle of bend is $4/5$ of a right angle, turn left) for instance, so that's quite a slow corner, or on a fast corner '100, 2, left' (in 100 metres, angle of bend is $2/5$ of a right angle, turn left), and then it goes straight into a '1, right' quite quickly so you have to know what's coming up. Worst-case scenario you have '100, flat-out, 1, right' and then they turn the page over and call '30, 90 degrees, left' and you have to slam on the brakes! You need to know that one way before, which comes with experience. You work together as a team and have to trust him when he says 'flat-out'.

Flat-out is about 120 miles per hour. Which is fast enough. You don't really want to go much faster than that. You can gear the car up to go faster, but then they are more out of control. You also get better acceleration when you gear them lower.

You want a car that is light, fast and can go further. The power to weight ratio is very important and comes down to fuel economy. Our Bowler Nemesis, for example, takes about 990 pounds of fuel – half a tonne – in a two-and-a-half-tonne car. So about a fifth of the weight is fuel. It makes a huge difference. The cars I usually race are about 2,425 pounds with 80–110 pounds of fuel; hardly anything at all. If you can get the economy down it makes a big difference. And when you start with it full of fuel it's like a great lumbering bus at the beginning of the day.

I also did the big rallies – the rally raids, like the Paris–Dakar, UAE desert challenge, Australia – there are rally raids all over the world. They can be a week or two long and every day you have one big, long stage –

about 500 miles a day on average – and that's on rough tracks and sand dunes. You can do it as long as you don't break down or get stuck. That's when you start running out of time. If you break something you've got to repair it or wait for support. You could be out there all night.

The Dakar is about three weeks with one rest day. So that's a tall order. Once we started at 7 a.m., broke the transmission about 6 p.m. – so we'd already been driving about ten hours – and then had to wait for the support truck which came about two in the morning, repair it and then had to drive on through the rest of the stage. We finished at 5.45 a.m. – just before the cut-off time – grabbed some breakfast and went out for the next day. Literally no sleep at all and up for 48 hours, concentrating.

A lot of the driving is blind out there. You can't recce it in advance, it's too long, so you never know what's going to happen. You have to have faith in the notes they give you and also faith in the co-driver to give you the right information when you need it because if he loses a page or gets lost, you've got to have total honesty. They have to say, 'I'm lost. Don't take anything I say now as certain, I've got to find my bearings again.' Then you have to find a landmark to work to, reset all your trip meters and carry on again. There's nothing worse than him saying, 'Yeah, you're OK, carry on' and then BANG! You hit a cross-rut or something.

We did the Dubai one a couple of years ago and we were doing quite well when my navigator said, 'You can really go for it now if you want.' We went over a couple of nasty sand dunes and you gauge them as you go along – a bit like waves. You can't see; you just guess and read the sand; you see the ripples, you see where it's more dense, you can see where the grip might be. You can read it a lot but they can catch you out and I misread one slightly! I thought it went down gently the other side, but it went down a lot and there was another jump straight after which we hit quite hard…

THE RALLY DRIVER

There was a big yelp and my navigator passed out cold. So I stopped and immediately called for medical assistance on the GPS and we got a helicopter to come and take him away. We think he passed out with the pain; he'd broken a vertebra in his back. Quite worrying when things like that happen. It goes through your mind – is he dead? I broke his hand last time we were out in Morocco, but he loves it. He loves the sport and if you are stuck in a car with someone for a long time you have got to get on with them.

On the rally raids, it helps to be older and more experienced and a little bit more slowly catchy monkey. You might look and think, 'It's going to be a nightmare over there,' you can see people getting stuck, so you slow down and calm down. It's not so frantic. You maybe don't need to hit the next checkpoint for 15 miles, so you pick a good route through. Everyone else may be getting stuck and so you choose to poodle round. They may come and overtake you again but then later on you see them upside-down and broken.

The same people who run the Dakar organise the Tour de France. There are similarities such as rolling stages; so when you drive, say, 500 miles and get to the end of a stage, everything's got to be there. The services, medics and doctors, spares, food for several thousand people. The top guys will set off early in the morning, while some drivers are just getting in from the previous day if they've had problems. You've still got to go in and have breakfast and maybe fix the car while the top team may be finished by lunchtime if they're really good, so another camp has to be set up further ahead, on a rolling basis. They have aircraft transporting too – like Hercules – so most of the bivouacs are now on old disused airfields throughout Africa. You have to take your own tent and you sleep anywhere; they lay carpets down over the sand.

Some of the stages also have quite a long liaison to get to the next stage. You may have long, dusty stretches, perhaps going down a dried-up riverbed for 75 miles and you're just meandering, droning away, hot and tired and it's at the end of the stage. That's when you get a lot of the accidents happening – on the liaison.

I've done a bit of rally race motor-biking, but I'm not that good. I love it though! A lot of it is about attitude and courage, but at club level they can come away with broken legs and broken arms because they are trying too hard. There are always people dying in that too. It's crazy; my other half has banned me from doing it! I did one World Championship rally raid in Tunisia and there were ten of us on bikes from the British contingent. All amateurs with one guy looking after us and only four of us made it to the finish. We had a broken back, broken arm, broken leg and heat exhaustion. So it's a high attrition rate. Only 130 finished out of 260 and I finished 130th! But I did finish. I'd like to do more of that. Generally one or two died every year in the Paris–Dakar on the bikes. There's a drivers' briefing every night with thousands of people in this huge bivouac where they feed everyone and in the briefing there's inevitably a minute's silence for a biker. It's the risk they choose to take.

But then the older you get, you do slow down a little bit so you have to go for it when you're young. You shouldn't wait until you've got more money – you're scared then. The determination and fire in your belly that gives you the edge diminishes when you get older; most definitely. Which is why the Formula One boys don't look old enough to drive. It's not recklessness as such, you don't care so much. On the really intense F1 racing and rallying you need that edge.

You can take off sometimes, over a bump. The easier ones are short tracks – like at Goodwood – when you take off the same bump loads of times and get familiar with it or when you are doing the same stage several times, like in Rally GB. With the longer ones, you only hit a bump once. The art is reading it, knowing how fast you can drive the car and hitting it right. It's not all flat-out. With bumps you have to ease off.

THE RALLY DRIVER

Gauging it is the key. When you are younger you may go at it 100 per cent, but that's when a big accident may happen – which we've had lots of – where we were far too fast and hit a tree, or when you land out of control, hit the back corner, smash it and you're out. There's a competitive streak in everybody.

There are good drivers and there are bad drivers. The only way you know who the bad drivers are is when you're racing. There's a lot of people who just wouldn't know what to do when the car is in a skid; 99 per cent of people on the road. The more you do, the younger you do it, the more you learn how to react, how to skid. Kids on go-karts or buggies who get the back drifting out either have no idea what to do or immediately put the opposite lock on. It's a reflex. Some things you just can't teach. It's intuitive.

You never know quite what's going to happen. The excitement, the different stages, they're never the same. You never get used to the stages. What the corner's going to do. It's all different. You may have never driven there – across Africa or something. You get to travel across the world and see some amazing sights, off the beaten track. The excitement of not knowing what's coming up.

Then the great thing is the reaction at the end. When you come off a stage, they have a board up with all the times of the cars and when you come through the finish – you do a flying finish usually and have a 328-foot slow down – you go, 'Yeah, that was great! Well done! That was brilliant!' and you breathe and let everything out even after only 20 minutes of racing. Then you look at the time and if you've knocked 15 seconds off the previous chap or you're the fastest by a long way, that gives you a buzz. Because they are all going, 'Cor, I can't believe that! How did you get it so fast?' It's just years and years of doing it. Trying to find every second off the time.

STORY TOLD BY ALEX

Six people were killed during the 1988 Dakar rally; three participants and three local residents. Racers were also blamed for starting a wildfire that caused a panic on a train running between Dakar and Bamako, where three more people died.

To date, about 58 people, including 24 competitors, have died in the Dakar Rally.

In 1982, Mark Thatcher, son of ex-British Prime Minister Margaret Thatcher, disappeared for six days on the Dakar rally. On 9 January, Mark, his French co-driver and a mechanic became separated from a convoy of vehicles after they stopped to make repairs. They were declared missing on 12 January. After a large-scale search, a plane from the Algerian military spotted their Peugeot 504 30 miles off the course. They were all unharmed.

THE RED ARROWS PILOT

Extreme rating: ☠☠☠☠☠
Danger level: ▁▁▄▄◼◼◼◼◻◻
Criteria: 1,500 flying hours (approximately eight years in the Royal Air Force); must have completed a frontline tour on a fast jet such as the Typhoon, Tornado, Harrier or Jaguar; assessed as an above-average pilot
Skills: Muscle memory; situational awareness; mental capacity; ability to debrief and learn continuously
Salary: £37,000–£44,000 (US $57,600–$68,500) as flight lieutenant, no extra salary for being in the Red Arrows

There are no reserve Red Arrows display pilots. There are only the nine. This is for safety reasons; spare pilots couldn't learn the nine positions to the standard required. 'Red 10' flies everywhere with us; he's not actually a display pilot but our road manager and does all the commentary. We generally transit (from display to display) as ten jets. Red 10 flies our spare. There are also 85 support personnel, who are known as 'The Blues' and they all wear blue flying suits. Each pilot flies for three years and has a nominated BAE Systems Hawk T1 Jet with their name on the side and a dedicated engineer. The engineers who fly in the back seats during the display season are known as the 'Circus'.

If you're not used to it, it's quite claustrophobic in the jet. It's relatively small and quite disorientating. The canopy is low; you've got a helmet and visor, an oxygen mask, life jacket and anti-g trousers on. The anti-g trousers give you about 2–2½-g tension, which helps when you may be pulling 7 or 8-g in a manoeuvre.

The show is in two halves. The first half is close formation flying; flying in different shapes in formation from the leader. The second half is more dynamic with jets doing individual manoeuvres. So the first half is difficult to get really precise, the second half is where you do more difficult manoeuvres often with other aircraft in close proximity.

The distance to each other is about 12–15 feet. There's one manoeuvre that we used to fly, the 'Apollo', which is 8–10 feet. That definitely concentrates the mind. The opposition pair – with the jets pointing at each other – are only 100 feet apart. So we train flying above a runway in Cyprus which is 100 feet wide. That helps with pattern recognition, getting it to be unconscious. If you do that all winter, three times a day, five days a week, you get used to the picture of what 100 feet looks like. In training, when the two jets are pointing at each other, one of them's the leader and one's the subordinate. The leader's job is to fly the pattern – to make the pattern work, the subordinate's job is to miss it and make it look good. You can only have one jet avoiding.

'Synchro' is the call sign of the opposition pair. 'Gypo' is the back four including the Synchro pair. 'Enid' – named after the Famous Five – is the five jets in front.

We fly most of the show at an average speed of 330 knots – about 380 miles per hour. The aircraft has an optimum turning performance due to the combination of speed and gravity. So you want to fly at a speed that is exciting, with enough energy to do vertical manoeuvres, but not so fast that the crowd can't see you. Faster than that and your manoeuvres would have to get bigger, which takes you further away from the crowd.

When you are flying in close formation you are looking directly at the other jet. When you are doing the dynamic stuff, you can't really be looking at the other jet, it's all happening too quickly, but you use your peripheral vision. You can sense if things aren't right. I know this sounds cheesy, but you don't have time to think. This is particularly true of fast jet flying – you have insufficient time to do a rational analysis of a situation. You have to be able to recognise the situation and go with your judgement and experience rather than try to analyse the 15 variables.

You do your most advanced manoeuvres in your third year, when you do the opposition passes. You have got a lot of experience at this stage, so you are more competent at the job.

In the first year, when you have the least experience to fall back on, there are two manoeuvres that are the most difficult to learn. One is called the 'Twizzle', and the reason this is so difficult is because it is a continuous rolling and pulling manoeuvre simultaneously. It's not that fast, but everything is changing in all three dimensions continuously. You increase your roll rate, you get inside the manoeuvre, you pull west; all the manoeuvres are interrelated and until you have seen it a gazillion times – over a whole season – and got used to the picture, it's difficult to fly well and make it look special.

Secondly, in terms of sheer terror and real concentration of the mind, we have a manoeuvre called the 'Rollback', where five jets fly together in a 'V' with the leader just flying a straight line. The two closest to the leader pull up and do a roll around the other two, and then the next two do the same. The reason this one's difficult is because we do it relatively slowly so the crowd can see it, probably around 280 knots, which is right at the edge of the aircraft's performance limit. They call it *nibbling the buffet*. Which means you are on the edge of your aircraft's capability. You have to fly it just on that edge. You have flying control, but in order to make a nice, tight, small manoeuvre, and because you are at such a slow speed, you have no extra capacity. You are on the edge of stalling and losing all performance and that's a bad thing!

With this manoeuvre, you pull up – right on the aircraft limit – and you go inverted on top of somebody else and you really have to complete the manoeuvre now. You can't break the manoeuvre down in bits; the first time you do it, it's for real and you do the whole thing. We practise a little bit higher at the start of training, but only at 500 feet. You don't want to go too much higher because the air is less dense and you'll lose performance.

So, in your first year, when you are still on a steep learning curve, you are rolling around another jet in very close proximity, right at the aircraft's performance limit – it's very difficult. The first time you see it, it's a nightmare; there's very little room for error. You go from being very excited about it and telling your mates down the pub that you're going to be a Red Arrows pilot and what a cool job you've got, to suddenly facing the reality of it.

You have to get to a stage where the basics are completely nailed and you have enough mental capacity left to get the smoke on, have some awareness of the fuel, know what the next manoeuvre is and who's doing what. As an example, when you first train you may do a loop with only four jets and your smoke is not on. In the video debrief you can quite clearly hear 'smoke on go'. And you think; how did I not process that information? All you have to do is press a button, but your brain becomes maxed out. When the skill becomes semi-conscious, then you start to develop some spare mental capacity. So in the first year, it's all you can do to stay in the right position with the smoke on. In the third year you are doing that, as well as flying at 100 feet, pulling 7 or 8 g and filing your flight plan on the radio for your transit out of the show!

Everyone who flies with the Red Arrows is already an experienced fighter pilot with quite a lot of experience in formation flying, but suddenly you are flying to an incredibly precise degree. The formation aspect is far more complex than anything you've done before. So you have to learn the basic skill set and maybe start flying within a box that is 5 or 6 square feet and get it down to within 1 square foot or less maybe.

We don't exactly measure these things but the basic idea is to go from being a complete idiot to getting it precisely right. So that's hard. The skill acquisition.

Although displays are complex and fast and you are at a different location every day, by the time you do them you have trained all winter, so you are in a groove. Where you are more likely to have some interesting moments is when you do something that's non-standard, like transits. You might think transits are routine, but actually flying ten jets through major civil airports and international airspace in all sorts of different weather, quite often operating close to the fuel limits… that's more likely to cause problems than anything during the display.

We did a transit once from Riyadh to Hurghada which is quite a long leg. We were flying at 40,000 feet – in a jet stream – in high level winds which were a lot stronger than forecast and picking up a dust storm, so we couldn't land at Hurghada or the diversion airport, Sharm el-Sheikh, and we were getting quite close to our minimum fuel line.

Now, in Saudi Arabia with ten jets, you have very limited landing options. It's not like flying over the UK where you have an extensive choice of airports. In the end, the leader decided to land at a tiny domestic airport called Wajh. This is basically an 8,000-foot strip of concrete near the sea, on the edge of the desert, with nothing else. No navigational aids. It only exists to serve some oilfields nearby so when there is a flight coming in with all the workers, they staff the airfield; the rest of the time, they have a bloke sat in a fire truck.

So we tell Saudi air traffic that we are diverting to Wajh and they are slightly confused but just let us get on with it. We also send one of us on to talk to Wajh on the radio and all he gets is an off-duty fireman, who clearly has absolutely no idea what he's talking about. And we have to find Wajh which is starting to disappear into the sandstorm too.

Despite all this we manage to navigate down and overfly the airfield at 500 feet to have a look. The one guy is sat there in his fire truck, having had some crazy conversation about red arrows, and then ten jets fly over at 500 feet, turn 270 degrees and brake to descend. We go down the runway one jet at a time, landing individually. The dust is getting sufficiently bad by then that when we're downwind, positioning to turn in and land, we can't see the runway. So we just fly in following the jet in front. We all land safely.

But by now of course the fireman has been on the phone to the local army unit about some crazy red jets that have landed from nowhere and the army meet us at the jets. They are polite and professional but they have guns and from the limited dialogue that we have, they basically say, 'You are coming with us, to sit in a room, while somebody outside sits with a rifle, until we work out what to do about you'.

Once they cleared all that up, they looked after us very well and we all had tea.

But certainly, landing in the middle of an unknown airfield in Saudi Arabia, when they are not expecting you, is not something you plan to do with ten military fighter jets from another country!

We once did some training in Moron, Spain and it was the worst one for bird strikes. Not only did it have quite a large bird population because of the local fields and harvesting, it was bad timing for the numbers of birds and they were quite big. So, we do a manoeuvre called the 'Corkscrew', where the Synchro pair fly straight down the runway, one inverted on top of the other, and myself and Red 8 contra-rotate around each other's smoke. We start about 30 feet from each other and once I begin rolling I just rely on Red 8 to keep position.

Rather than actually look at the separation, you get a gut feeling using your peripheral vision and a sense for what is about right. Then you are constantly making small adjustments whilst you are rolling, doing a manoeuvre upside-down and close to the smoke. Whilst I am inverted, and on the third roll going over the smoke, I hear a massive thump and straight away I know it's a bird strike.

Your instant thought then is, *I hit a bird, I don't know what the damage could be*. The most likely problems after a bird strike are: loss of control, loss of the engine, maybe a punctured wing which could lead to a fuel or hydraulic leak or it's caused some handling damage. So a bird strike is not so bad as long as the engine's still going and you're flying straight but it can lead to other problems that aren't obvious straight away. You need to deal with it quickly, find out what's wrong without getting too far away from the airfield, get some height, make sure the aircraft handles OK at a lower speed (because you have to land at a lower speed) and get it on the ground.

If you were on your own, that would be enough to make your day interesting.

The other variables here, however, are that you are just rolling out of being inverted at 300 feet and it's my last roll. What happens in practice is that the Synchro leader radios 'smoke off go' and that's the signal for the end of the manoeuvre for Gypo. The significance of that is we no longer have control of the radio.

The section flying in front of the crowd is the one that has use of the radio for safety reasons. And nobody else can speak. So when he calls 'smoke off go', it's the handover of the radio and I can't speak. The main section – Enid – are now running into their next manoeuvre and they are about to start calling over the radio. So if I say something at the same time as a critical radio call, while they're doing a manoeuvre, it has enormous safety implications for them. They are also in control of the runway.

So it's about mental capacity and situational awareness. Having a model in your mind about what's going on.

What you want to do is get away from the formation, get some height, say something on the radio and take ownership of the runway. So you have to have some awareness and self-discipline. Balance the priorities. If you were just flying on your own, your only priority would be your own life, followed by the jet. But because you are flying in this environment, your priorities are actually the crowd first, followed by the rest of the formation, followed by you. Now obviously you have a high degree of self-preservation, but you have to work out the priorities.

This is why you need people with a certain level of experience. You can teach the motor skills of flying, but what you need experience for is this sort of stuff. The situational awareness and mental capacity when it doesn't go so well.

So I broke away from the formation and started doing my checks to come into land, but didn't actually say anything on the radio. I'm familiar with Enid's manoeuvres and I know the exact sequence of their radio calls, so when I know there is a decent gap, I quickly say: 'Nine's got a bird strike, I'm positioning to land.' At which point Enid then stop their manoeuvre safely, brake off and give me the runway.

So on one level, a bird strike is not the end of the world, but like all these things, because of the context where you have nine jets, flying very fast, close to the ground, each doing different things, it's never quite as simple as it looks. There are lots of variables at play.

Then you get the random things that aren't particularly dangerous. We did a fly past over the Millennium Stadium in Cardiff for the World Cup Final. We went over it, right on time, right down the middle, in very demanding conditions and when we landed back at Scampton, I said to the leader, 'You did a good job there, that was quite demanding.' And he said, 'Yeah, I was quite pleased with myself, but you'd have thought if they were so excited about it, they'd have left the bloody roof open!'

One aspect that goes hand in hand with the professionalism is the mutual trust involved. It seems obvious on a superficial level – flying close to each other, in formation, yes, you are trusting the others to not be crap and to be in the right position, but equally you have an element of control over your own destiny. You could get out of someone's way if you really needed to or if it all went crazy – it's relatively unlikely, in formation, that somebody would crash into you that you had no awareness about beforehand. Where it becomes much more of a factor, when there is real trust, is when you are relying on other people's professional standards to be doing exactly what they are supposed to be doing when you can't see them.

So to give you an example, you have the Synchro pair who fly towards each other; pointing at each other. The Synchro leader's job is to fly the pattern, to position the cross in front of the middle of the crowd. Synchro two's job is to make the pass look good and miss him. So that's a relatively straightforward concept, but the execution of that is a whole lot more complicated than it sounds. Because what's going on is that there are constant adjustments being made to correct errors in the previous pattern or wind errors on the day. The pattern is subtly different if the wind is blowing due east than blowing due west. If somebody is flying into the wind, they will have to extend a bit to go further, somebody flying downwind will have to go less and this is all happening at 360 miles per hour, at 100 feet, at a live show, using a map and a stopwatch!

So even on a perfect gin-clear day, it's quite complicated to make that happen right in the middle of the crowd every time because of these tiny corrections being made on the radio like 'extend by half a second'. Take your perfect day and add 30 knots of wind – there are some decent sized corrections you have to make. And now add in 3 miles visibility.

When you are at opposite ends of the pattern, you can't see each other. So what you do is fly in towards the meeting place and use a feature on the ground as a timing threshold. If you both reach the threshold at the same time, you are going to meet in the middle. But if it's a really murky day, you may lose sight of the other person. So now, the leader is flying along, the other jet's coming in at 360 miles per hour – so they are closing at 720 miles per hour – and he may suddenly see the other jet pointing exactly at him and it doesn't appear to be correcting. This is all happening quite quickly and he thinks the other jet's going to hit him. What does he do? He has to hold his pattern.

There may be some micro last second chance to save yourself as you think, 'Oh my God we are definitely going to crash', but basically he has to trust the other guy to make the correction. Because if the leader makes a correction and the other jet makes a counter-correction, it's a potential disaster. So no matter how bad it looks, he has to trust that the other pilot is going to do the right thing at his end.

Another simple example is where Chris and I flew Red 8 and 9 and the rejoin is a lot more complicated than the stuff you are doing in front of the crowd. We'd come off at either end of the runway, we'd both turn behind the crowd towards each other, Chris would fly at 1,000 feet and I would fly at 500 feet and we can't use the radio because somebody else is in front of the crowd, so he would put a little bit of blue smoke on, and I would double click my radio to say that I'd seen him.

Now on a bad day, I can't see him. So I turn and hold my line and we've got to get together for the next manoeuvre which is due to happen in 20 seconds. So I'm halfway down the runway, in murky conditions, I roll at 500 feet, pulling 8-g and start doing a flat turn. There is an assumption here in my mind that he is at 1,000 feet. Now that might sound obvious, but there's a lot going on here. I'm turning blind and I have to catch up and rejoin him. So I turn and I am trusting him to be in the right position.

And 500 feet sounds like a lot, but when you are flying at those speeds, it's not much at all. We only need to be each 250 feet out – a couple of seconds' climb or descent. So there are a lot of situations like that, where it's not quite perfect, it's not quite what it should be, but you've got to grit your teeth, show a bit of balls and fly procedurally in the trust and assumption that the other person is also flying in a predictable, professional way and is procedurally doing their thing as well.

Where trust is really stretched is where it's blind trust and the consequences are very significant.

If everyone's done what they're supposed to do, there's no risk; if anyone's deviated, there's massive risk. You trust they haven't deviated. You find out the real depth of your values. Your mental strength; the height of your professional standards.

It's this fine line; this balance of hanging in there and getting the job done and knowing the point in which actually it's not safe. The wrong side of that line has enormous consequences, and that's very subjective. You are looking for people who have the balls to go up to the line, but then the sense not to go over it. You can't measure those things in a selection process. You will get a better opinion of it by chatting to them in the pub.

And these guys have already stepped up to the plate. They've been flying fast jets and most have served in Afghanistan, so you're not really looking to test that, you are just trying to get a gut feeling on the 'fit'.

Most people who do the job are ordinary mates, who are in the job as fighter pilots, reasonably competent and a bit lucky being in the right place at the right time to get the job. They are not rock stars; they are generally reasonably grounded. It's just your job. They have quite a low awareness of the external view. It's not until afterwards they realise that the rest of the population think it's the coolest thing ever.

Money's not why people do it. You get paid what you get paid. You do it because you want to, like joining the military. The reward is not so much external recognition, which is nice, but because you are so challenged. It pushes you to the limits of your flying skills. It's very intrinsically rewarding when you get it right. It's cool because it's the most demanding flying you'll ever do. That's why you do it.

STORY TOLD BY RED 9

Two Red Arrows pilots died in separate accidents in 2011.

The Red Arrows fly Hawk aircraft capable of a top speed of Mach 1.2 (approx. 912 miles per hour). In a display they will perform manoeuvres just 100 feet from the ground, 12 feet away from each other, at 380 miles per hour and experience up to 8 g.

To counteract the g-force pilots wear anti-g suit which clamps the blood in the legs while simultaneously pilots tense their muscles to freeze the blood in the upper body. If they didn't they would most likely black out at 5 g. Red Arrows pilots pull 4 g about 30 times and maybe 7–8 g five times in a sortie, for three years.

THE SNIPER

Extreme rating: ☠☠☠☠☠
Danger level: ▁▁◢◢◢◼◼◼◼

Criteria: No formal qualifications required, training is provided; aged 16–33 in regular army or 17–43 in Territorial Army; physical fitness; semi-decent shot at long-range rifle marksmanship

Skills: Good tactical awareness; sense of direction; excellent field-craft skills (such as camouflage and concealment); patience; diligence; able to work quickly and accurately under pressure; self-reliant; decisive and motivated in difficult, dangerous, hostile and uncomfortable situations

Salary: £37,000 (US $57,600) basic salary for a sergeant, there is no extra pay for the qualification

I did an operational tour in Northern Ireland where the main impetus of the battalion was working against the PIRA (Provisional Irish Republican Army), the UVF (Ulster Volunteer Force) and the UDA (Ulster Defence Association) amongst others; normal, conventional/counter-insurgency warfare, but I worked as a sniper. Back then there was a sniper, believed to be American or American trained, working for the IRA who had killed about six or eight soldiers. I've got photos of the street signs saying 'sniper at work'. He used the big .50 calibre which has a range of 4,920–5,905 feet.

At the time, I knew a soldier who was on foot patrol with an RUC (Royal Ulster Constabulary) constable; the constable coughed and was dead before he hit the floor. It was that .50 cal. sniper who shot him and the cough was the constable taking his last breath. My friend was explaining how weird he felt because the sniper must have had both of them in his sights and it's like, 'Who do I dislike the most? The British Army or the Irish policeman?' Luckily for him and unluckily for the policeman, he chose the RUC. So he got killed and that was that. They knew it was him from the hole that the .50 cal left on his body, centre chest. He died instantly.

I also worked in Bosnia as a sniper. Once you've got the qualification, you can be called upon wherever you are; you don't have to be within a sniper platoon. Whenever we deployed anywhere, I just grabbed my sniper rifle and then if we needed it, it was there. Ireland, Bosnia and Iraq were peacekeeping tours. When we went to Iraq, the CO (commanding officer) wasn't even going to take the rifles, thinking they wouldn't be needed, but we ended up using them a lot. Either you're caught in that particular time in history, or you're not. It being a peacekeeping tour, you're more or less walking around as a police officer.

We do lots of different jobs, but you don't necessarily pull the trigger. You mostly use your eyes and ears doing reconnaissance or long-distance observation for the battle group. The second role is to take out priority targets.

In the Spearhead Battalion, a high-readiness, short-notice unit, you're on standby to go somewhere if there's a problem. So you can't drink, can't go farther than a certain travel time from base, and you might get a phone call 'Come to the barracks now', then maybe get straight on the chopper to Ireland. I've done that a few times and worked against different people, but never actually shot any of them.

Until Iraq, and then I made up for it.

I went out to Iraq in 2004 as part of an infantry battalion on a peacekeeping tour, essentially to win hearts and minds and to create conditions for the rebuilding of Iraq, but ended up fighting for my life in a situation as outnumbered and desperate as Rorke's Drift. I completed a six-month tour as the platoon commander of a sniper platoon of 18 men, isolated, besieged and under constant fire. Our base was CIMIC House in a town called Al Amarah, 150 miles north of Basra.

Whatever type of operation you go on, before you even get settled in, there's work to be done with maps, air photography – or if you can get a fly-over in a heli, even better. Because you've got to know what's around you; the lie of the land. If you don't do your homework you could shoot someone and then run straight into an enemy sentry position you haven't even looked at. There's a lot of work involved, especially if you're behind enemy lines and there's only a few of you.

My job one day early on in the tour was checking in at the different police stations in Al Amarah. We went to one police station and, rather unusually, weren't getting anything out of them, so I departed – backwards – down the path and then they all came out. I could tell a difference in the mood straight away. You have a mental adjustment that it's gone wrong. You pick up on the atmospherics and that's why I was walking backwards. You don't take your eyes off them; you can't trust them for a second. These people don't like you and they have a particular mentality. They don't care if they die that day and trying to overcome that mentality is crazy. But that's what you're up against.

It all kicked off from there and the next thing, a grenade came over the wall and we could hear rifles being cocked behind the gates and people running to preset firing positions. I knew it was going to kick off, I just knew it. I've done enough tours to know.

So as the platoon commander I had to pull it out of the bag.

I got everybody into position and then I saw this guy with a weapon sneaking up on us. I put three rounds into him. First kill. And then everything went absolutely mental. There were enemies everywhere; in the compound, on the roofs, shooting down at us. They had an advantage. If you fight Arabs, you learn very quickly that you've got to get up high. So after our first few battles, you know to kick someone's door in, go up on the roof and fight on the rooftops. It takes away the advantage if you're on the same level and we've generally got better weapons.

At the end of the day, we were sent there to do a job, it went bad and we reacted as we saw fit. If anything, we were pleased that we gave a good account of ourselves and all the guys in the camp, to the last person, were *really* swearing because they'd wanted to be on that patrol. From then on, until the next lot got shot at, everyone looked at us in awe. It was weird. I was pleased that I'd finally done it and not been found wanting.

We grabbed the roof at our main base, CIMIC House, straight away; it was the highest viewpoint, and we built another platform up top with sangars (temporary fortifications). I could lie there with five different weapons at my disposal.

Weapons-wise, you've got your normal infantry weapon: the SA80. That's your standard 5.56-millimetre assault rifle with a range of 980–1,640 feet. We used a couple of machine guns: the GPMG 7.62 millimetre (general purpose machine gun, or Gimpies). That's a medium machine gun which replaced the Bren gun. And the Minimi, with a folding butt. That's a 5.56 as well, so the calibre's smaller than the GPMG. We had a sniper rifle as well, the 7.62-calibre L96, known as the 'long'.

The sniper rifle is a single-shot, bolt action weapon, so you have to feed each round into the chamber and then fire it off. 'One shot, one kill' is an adage that comes from the training and the accuracy of it. The sniper weapons are point of aim, point of impact. So you actually bring the fall of shot onto the crosshair's centre instead of 'aiming off'. Sniper rifles are built for range; the further away from the enemy, the safer you are. Obviously the better the sights, the more accurate they are and that's before you go into windage and elevation and all that sort of stuff. It was made by a British company, Accuracy International, which is based in Portsmouth.

Our sniper rifles have deflection and elevation drums. They're very similar and, along with the focus, you adjust them and it's like you're looking at the guy right *there*. You set one for the strength of the wind, which counteracts any deflection on the bullet, and which also depends on distance to the target. With the elevation, there are various methods of judging the distance from firer to target. When you have that worked out, you set the elevation drum to the distance required. Once you have set the sight to the distance, and deflected the strength of the wind, you will know exactly where that round will fall.

You've also got to have a stable firing position and be comfortable. This isn't massively scientific, but you've gotta get it right, otherwise you might miss.

We also use range cards. Instead of doing all the maths when you should be shooting, you'll work out the range to some key places; likely positions that might come into play. So maybe a bridge or, if you know the target's going to come to a certain building and stand in the doorway, you work out exactly the distance to that. You have all that worked out on your card and you'll name them, like 'red roof'. So instead of having to do that when the target's there, you've already done it. You can just say, 'red roof', look at your card, and go, 'OK, windage, so and so, range so and so,' it saves time. But also it breaks up the battlefield. You can, for example, reference the red roof and at three o'clock for another 300 feet, start shooting. It makes everything easier because you've got it all there already rather than lasering it and waiting for the wind calculations.

In assessing the wind, you still do the old 'pick up a bit of grass and throw it in the air', if there's grass there, and you look at everything around you the old-fashioned way – the tops of the trees, the grass, the flags. Flags are everywhere in Iraq, they're a very 'flaggy' nation.

We work in pairs; you have the Number One, who's the main shooter and he carries the sniper rifle, and the Number Two, who's his protection initially, carrying a standard infantry rifle for more local targets. As soon as you get on location, you're looking for the target. You check the area as you're moving in, especially if you're behind enemy lines. Households out there are allowed one weapon per house after the ceasefire, which is really crazy, but they've always had weapons because it's a cut-throat sort of place. At nights, you may have the old guy of the house sat on the roof, as a normal family person, but armed. Everyone would be doing this. So it was really hard differentiating between somebody just sitting on his roof, protecting his property as you patrol past, or 'Is that guy with a weapon aiming it at me?' It's another thing you have to consider before you open fire.

While you're focused on that, your Number Two sets up sights with a handheld scope and does the windage, elevation and range calculations. So while you're getting yourself comfortable to fire, he'll relay to you: 'Yeah, OK, we've been here before and it's red four, so you need to set it to that.' But obviously the wind and light changes, it's a royal pain. It makes a target bigger or smaller and the heights harder to calculate…

You're speaking to each other all the time, both confirming what you can see. You probably have radio traffic coming in as well, because in different scenarios, you might not be allowed to shoot until a certain thing has happened or a certain time has arrived. You don't do a running commentary; you say what needs to be said and that's it. The rest of the time, you're focusing on what you're doing. And for both One and Two, you spend your life looking through things. So Number One's looking through his scope and Number Two's looking through binos or his scope, and you're speaking to each other: 'Can you see that on the left?' 'Yeah, there's a woman with a kid walking down so and so, car going left to right, gunman in the alleyway, someone on the roof there, can't see what he's doing…' Just talking about stuff. And you slow your breathing down.

When we were fighting in Iraq, most of our sniping was opportunity shooting; so any act of aggression we saw, we shot them. I would work out for instance: 'He's about to put a mortar round in that tube, therefore he's having more effect than the guy that's giving him the rounds' so I'd shoot him first. You're there because he's doing something bad. He's trying to kill you or he's going to kill others.

If you were fighting the Taliban – as I did a couple of years ago – you may have a priority target list and maybe a grainy old photo to ID somebody. For Iraq, we had a 'Who's Who' Most Wanted pack of cards which helped troops on the ground when they were doing checkpoints, looking for people. If you were in a sangar, you'd have them on a wall or under a bit of perspex to keep them clean and think, 'Oh, yeah, that's so and so.' Very similar in Northern Ireland but they were printed on one sheet. We used to have gold, silver and bronze targets: they are always prioritised.

I personally don't know anyone with their own tally of how many they've killed. When you're sniping you've got a sniper's logbook but in Iraq we didn't keep a log. As platoon commander, after every contact, I interviewed each member of my platoon and asked them: 'How many do you think you shot? Do you think you killed any? Do you think you wounded any?' It was also a way of defusing or de-stressing the guys in the battles. Because they were killing a lot of people. I worked out we had just over 200 confirmed kills as a group of 18 – which includes the drivers. It's a lot. Most of us were on 20-plus kills.

Generally, people who have done it for real don't brag about that sort of thing. Every time you pull the trigger, if you hit the guy you're pleased, but for many of the situations we found ourselves in, we didn't have time to think. We just had to go on to the next target. It was crazy. You'd get a pause in the battle and you're like, *'Whew,'* have a quick drink, a pee, and then get on with it again.

As it went on, we got more and more experience. We were the go-to platoon for any high-risk location; if they wanted something done and knew there was going to be fighting, they'd go on red alert – then I'd be the first one through the door: 'Let's go, boys. We're on!'

You can either do it or you can't. There are very few people that are good enough. Not just because of the shooting, but because of the enemy element. You've got to be good at concealing yourself. That's the hardest skill. For example, when you're doing the training, someone would be sat on a chair with a set of binos and a stopwatch, and 12 to 20 of us with our ghillie suits on, in an open field, would have 30 seconds to run and hide. And you've gotta sprint hell for leather. So while he's stood there talking, you're scanning around looking for something to conceal yourself... a little dip in the ground, a trapped shadow... The basics of a good fire position are a good screen and a good backdrop so you can conceal yourself between the two; a shadow that you can hide in or something the same colour as you.

If you stand in a field or near some woods and see how things are growing – in particular, trees and bushes – look within the base and you'll see the darker areas. They're called 'trapped shadows'; darkness is trapped deep in the bushes, behind trees, in-between trees, in-between vegetation and stuff like that. So if you're wearing the right colours, you can place yourself in there and you're virtually invisible. Until you start shooting. Then, as you're moving, you try to find a good backdrop and a good screen in front of you; that's why you can't go in a straight line. You may go into a dip in the ground, and then conceal yourself along a ditch to get from A to B, and then crawl across a bit and into the water... you're trying to conceal yourself the whole way and not be silhouetted in open ground. If you have to crawl and take an hour to an inch, then that's what you have to do.

The worst thing was getting shot twice in a month. In an ambush I got shot in the left shoulder; the bullet went through all my kit and clothing, hitting my shoulder blade, luckily only penetrating a few millimetres, and I was in a cemetery – so that was quite emotional. I managed to shrug it off because I was the boss and if I'd have behaved unusually, I think some of the younger lads would have crumbled. About a month later, a round deflected off the back of my helmet when I was on the roof. But all I could do was throw another sandbag behind me and carry on. Luckily I had my helmet on.

We could have been killed every day, a hundred times a day. I still wonder now how the hell we got out of there in one piece.

I was glad to get on the plane out of there. While you're there, you're working 100 per cent at the job. But as soon as you get told, 'Stop that now, hand your stuff in, you're going to go,' then you can't wait. There were a hundred times I thought I'd never be flying out of there.

STORY TOLD BY SERGEANT M.

In Iraq, in 50°C and during a 23-day period, Sergeant M's platoon (amongst others) were on the receiving end of 595 mortar rounds (26 a day on average) during 230 separate bombardments. They were also assaulted with 57 RPGs (rocket propelled grenades) and five 107-millimetre rockets. The platoon fought against an estimated 500 militia, were involved in 25 firefights in town and repelled 86 ground assaults on their base in what has been described as the lengthiest defensive stand since World War Two. The battalion suffered two fatalities and over fifty casualties.

The longest recorded sniper kill currently stands at 8,120 feet by a sniper from the Household Cavalry of the British Army against the Taliban in 2009 using an Accuracy International L115A3 long-range rifle. It likely took six seconds to reach its target.

THE SOLO ROUND-THE-WORLD YACHTSMAN

There are two types of extreme day when sailing around the world. There is 'extreme day' as most people see it, which is actually 'extreme weather': really rough; really windy; the boat's bouncing around and it's like being inside a washing machine. From a racing perspective, however, it's not so extreme because you are just in a survival situation. You hang on to the boat, hang on to yourself, try not to fall over the side, try not to break anything and ride the storm out. It looks extreme; it is rough; it's what's perceived as a really extreme day, but it's not. From a sailing point of view it's just challenging.

The really extreme days are when the weather is constantly changing; in light or strong winds. You hardly sleep – you are relentlessly checking the weather, checking the competition, checking the sails – trimming them incessantly. Every time the wind changes strength or direction you trim or change the sails and they could be up for just ten minutes before the wind changes again. So the sail has to come back down and another goes up. It's tough. It's physically very demanding. From a sailing perspective, it's not an extreme day when the weather is stormy but when it is changeable.

The worst wind I've been out in is 70 knots which is over 80 miles an hour. If you imagine standing on the roof of your car speeding down the motorway at 80 miles an hour – that's what it's like standing on the deck of a boat. Only it's wet, at a 45-degree angle and bouncing around. Forty to forty-five degrees is quite typical when it's really rough… or 90 degrees when it's capsized, or 180 degrees and upside-down if it's gone really wrong!

Deep down in the Southern Ocean, you may get snow which makes the deck icy and slippery, so that's something else to be careful of, but the Southern Ocean is a great place to go sailing – like nowhere else on earth. It's unique. The weather and the waves roll around the planet down there, unchecked by land, so they get bigger and bigger. The storms also grow in intensity because there's nothing to break them up, so they spin around the bottom of the world, one after another, only a couple of days apart. It's an amazing, vast expanse of raw weather and mountainous seas down there, with no other shipping, no other human life – not even aircraft vapour trails in the sky – and just albatross to keep you company. Best place on the planet to go sailing!

On a very clear night you can see the dense belt of stars in the Milky Way and the aurora australis – the Southern Lights. There are all these shimmering colours: yellows, purples, greens and reds, like a net curtain flickering in the wind. It's awe-inspiring. Not many people get to see the Southern Lights.

I've also seen all sorts of wildlife: flying fish, whales, sharks, turtles, dolphins… I've had an octopus on deck and a seal that came and put his chin on the cockpit. You try and steer clear of whales. More often than not they stay away from you but if you're not running an engine they often don't know you're there. So sometimes yachts do run into them. Big whales probably wouldn't even know about it.

It's extremely cold down there. Obviously the further south you go and the closer to Antarctica you get, the colder it gets. When the wind is blowing from the south, it's coming straight off the ice sheet of Antarctica and the air temperature is well below −10°C plus the chill factor.

There is nothing worse than getting cold and once you get wet, you get cold. Then it's very, very hard to warm up again, your energy goes and you get ill. So the top priority is keeping as dry as you can and having the best kit available. We wear a layered system of clothing including Gore-Tex breathable base layers so the sweat wicks away from the body; otherwise it condenses and freezes on your skin. Also we wear drysuits, SealSkinz (waterproof socks), thermal balaclavas, mountaineering harnesses and helmets, diving gloves… we pull from other extreme sports to get the best kit. We also have big thick soles on our boots so we don't get the cold coming up from the deck.

Icebergs are monitored and tracked by satellite and iceberg reports are freely available online. The big icebergs aren't a problem because you can see those from a long way away. It's the small ones that break off – the growlers – that are dangerous. Some are the size of a small family hatchback and they float just below the surface – you can't see them. If you hit one at speed it will completely destroy the boat, but they always drift downwind of an iceberg, so you sail upwind of them.

Big waves aren't so much of a problem. I've sailed past a 72-foot wave, which is huge, but they're not usually breaking waves in the middle of the ocean. They are mountainous, but there might be a mile between crests so you tend to travel up and down them like a cork, rather than crashing through. When you get big changes in depth over a short distance, like the Bay of Biscay or around Cape Horn, where the depth goes from thousands to hundreds of feet, the water piles up and that's where you get big breaking waves and confused seas. They are much more dangerous.

I've been quite lucky; I've not had any broken bones. I've been bumped and bruised a lot. Rope burns occasionally, frostbite, cold, salt sores, but no major injuries. I know plenty of sailors who have broken arms, broken ribs, hips, fingers; it's a fairly common occurrence.

Boat damage includes broken rudders, broken masts, broken boom, broken spinnaker pole, lots of damaged sails, holes in the boat, capsized boat – all sorts! It's better to break the boat than break the person. The boat's easier to fix.

Medical kit depends on the environment and how long you are going to be at sea. On the round-the-world races where you are going to be at sea for a long time – maybe six months – you carry a very comprehensive medical kit and you have to learn how to use it. I will even carry intravenous morphine and sutures so I can stitch myself back together again.

From an injury perspective if you are close enough to the shore – no more than 150 miles away – a helicopter can come and pick you up. Other than that, in solo ocean racing you are very dependent on the rest of the fleet to be your emergency rescue service. If you hole the boat and start to sink, you are then relying on your competitors to come and help you out. There is a code of conduct for yacht racing where if you need to help a competitor, the racing stops. Racing is all good and well until you are in peril. If an emergency situation occurs, then the racing takes a back seat and you go to that person's aid and apply to get dispensation afterwards from the race committee.

You just have to take care; hang on to things; anticipate the motion of the boat. Don't put yourself in a risky situation. If you can do something safer, then you do; even if it takes a little longer to do it, especially with short-handed sailing – solo or two-handed.

The hardest thing I have to do is go up the mast. That's always a challenge. It's great going up there when the weather's not too bad because you can often see your competitors. But when you're bouncing around, it's hard; you get bruised and banged around up there. I often wear a mountaineering harness and helmet because you do get thrown around a lot. If the boat is rocking a little, up at the top of the mast it is rocking an awful lot more – that motion is magnified the farther up you go. So you clip on to the mast to avoid getting thrown out like a pendulum, otherwise you come back and hit it, which hurts – people break limbs up there quite often. So that's a tough job.

Pirates are more and more of a problem. Off the west coast of Africa and the north-east coast of Brazil there are pirate issues. You have to sail away and stay off shore; if you are 100 miles or so off shore and over the horizon they won't even know you are there. Pirates tend to go for the cruising yachts, gin palaces and motor boats, not the racing yachts which are worth a lot of money but not easy assets to turn into cash.

You do a sea survival course and learn about life rafts predominantly – how to survive at sea in one. Also how to limit damage to the boat and how to repair it so you can get to land under your own power, which is the aim. But if you have to abandon ship you learn how to get into a life raft – which isn't easy – and then how to survive in it because they are not great places to be. That's why we use the phrase 'always step *up* into a life raft'. It means by that point your boat has truly sunk. The last place you want to be is inside a life raft, even if you are sinking.

I would say sailors would score eight out of ten on a danger scale as it can be very dangerous. The biggest danger is being washed off the boat and drowning which is a very real risk, so you clip on. Falling overboard and drowning are big issues. Others are broken bones, broken ribs, exposure, frostbite, and so on. Being hit by the boom and caving in your skull, for the less experienced. It's a very dangerous environment; very volatile. You can't control it. You've got to make the most of it.

I love it.

STORY TOLD BY ALEX

 **DANGER FACT:**

In the 1998 Sydney–Hobart yacht race five boats sank and six people drowned. In the 1979 Fastnet yacht race there were 15 fatalities. Many people abandoned their boats and went into life rafts where they died of exposure or got washed out. Two days later their boats were found still floating.

 **EXTREME FACT:**

Francis Joyon holds the current non-stop, single-handed, multihull round-the-world sailing record. He completed it in 57 days, 13 hours, 34 minutes in 2008 in a 95-foot trimaran (eastward route). Dame Ellen MacArthur holds the female record of 71 days, 14 hours, 18 minutes in her B&Q sponsored trimaran (2005).

Michel Desjoyeaux holds the monohull record in 84 days, 3 hours, 9 minutes in January 2009 as part of the Vendée Globe race (eastward route).

The westward route is tougher and slower as it sails against the prevailing winds, waves and currents. The current single-handed monohull record is held by Jean Luc Van Den Heede, totalling 122 days, 14 hours, 3 minutes in 2004.

THE STORM CHASER

Extreme rating: ☠☠☠☠☠
Danger level: ▬▬▬■■■□□□□
Criteria: Meteorological training and research; knowledge of and experience with severe weather hurricanes, tornados, storms, etc; business acumen to run a tour agency, or analytical and forecasting skills to sell data and predictions to weather bureaus
Skills: Monitoring weather forecasts; locating and following storms; using meteorological equipment; collecting and analysing data; taking and selling photography and videos of storms; awareness of hazards and ability to stay safe; first aid; radio communications
Salary: US $18,000 (£11,300, average salary) to $100,000 (£63,000, running a successful storm-chasing agency)

I am a storm chaser. I have been chasing storms for 27 years.

I grew up in Kansas and when I was eight years old our house was levelled by an F5 tornado. (F is for Fujita scale; an F5 is described as an 'incredible tornado' with 261–318-mile-per-hour winds causing catastrophic damage.) Fortunately we were in the basement and survived but that piqued my interest in weather. I've been a weather buff all my life.

I run a storm-chasing tour company and I'm also a professional videographer and photographer. So all that combined kind of makes up who I am. We do scheduled tornado-chasing tours from early May through to the end of June. We do on-call tours where we maintain a list of people's emails who want to be notified any time that it looks like there's going to be severe weather, and we go down to the desert south-west and do photography tours of the cactus, canyons, monsoon storms, lightning and so forth. We also do hurricane-chasing tours in the fall. I took a group into the eye of Hurricane Katrina. We went to Taiwan and did a super typhoon about four or five years ago and have done a couple of hurricane chases down in Mexico. It's interesting. I broke the world record for the number of tornados that I've seen in my lifetime – I saw my 600th over the summer this last year.

Tornados still make my heart beat but if I get a big supercell thunderstorm and the storm structure is really pretty, that's as nice as a tornado in my opinion. You can get these big, majestic storms that look like spaceships; they really do. They look like a stack of dinner plates; five or six plates deep. They're big and round because of the wind shear causing them to rotate and you get magnificent structure. You hear the constant rumble of the thunder up aloft and lightning flashing and hitting the ground and then underneath you get a wall cloud that forms and a tornado. Like I said, I've seen over 600 tornados now and I act like it's the first one I ever saw. I get excited, I really do. So, yeah: tornados definitely still are my number one.

Waterspouts are really exciting. A totally different mechanism forms the waterspout versus a classic, supercellular tornado. But nonetheless, waterspouts are really neat.

My job is extremely dangerous. You never know what Mother Nature's going to do. I have more respect for a bolt of lightning than I do for anything else in severe weather because that's the one thing you cannot calculate: where a bolt is going to occur. I actually had a bolt hit my tripod; I was standing about 5 feet away and it melted my camera and knocked me down. That just gave me a very important sense of fear for lightning and tornados. When you have a tornado forming, you have to give it respect.

The most magnificent lightning that you'd ever come across is in the desert south-west in the United States during July and August in the monsoon season. You have to be able to position yourself where you get these magnificent long fork bolts coming out of high-base thunderstorms… it's just stunning. With the desert scenery – all the wildlife and cactus and mountains – when you get a bolt of lightning with the red rocks around, it turns the cloud base red. Those clouds are just absolutely gorgeous to look at.

A 'supercell thunderstorm' is a big, rotating thunderstorm and sometimes the storm structure is just absolutely mesmerising. You look at this thing and it's towering 70,000 feet above your head and it's as violent as violent can get. You can actually see the storm rotate and take on that spaceship look. It sometimes looks like a corkscrew; it just spirals up into the sky. You can see all the layers of clouds and watch this thing. It's humbling. I've had times where it's brought tears to my eyes, just watching the storm. It's such a spectacle of nature. You think of all the power that's involved in one of these big, violent thunderstorms.

This world that we live in is intense and it's so amazing to see the natural sights. Absolutely stunning.

Some of these storm chasers just get way, way too close; one of them rolled his vehicle about three weeks ago in a freak tornado in Oklahoma. You can have a really strong gust of wind wrap around the tornado. You can have a tree or a house literally come out of the sky. I've seen stuff like that. If you don't respect Mother Nature, Mother Nature is gonna getcha. People are going to die. That's pretty much the way it works. I think my job is very dangerous, between big hailstorms, tornados, lightning and flooding. You have to be on your guard, at all times.

I take people into the 'core' of the thunderstorm, where the heavy rain and hail falls. I want my guests to see what a baseball-size hailstone looks like hitting the ground and be able to get out and pick one up and see what it looks like after the hail stops falling. I want them to see what winds blowing at 80, 90, 100 miles per hour look like from the ground draft of a thunderstorm. I want to get them close enough to a tornado so they can see the debris fly and they can feel the rumble of the tornado in their chest.

We have 15-passenger vans and we buy them to beat up and destroy. The hailstones can break the windshield so we always park the cars so that only the windshield gets broken and not the side or back windows. The front windshield has safety glass in it so if a big chunk of ice hits, it'll generally just crack it.

We have GPS and radar in every one of our vans so we can watch the path the storm or tornado is moving in and position ourselves to move right along with it. Typically, a tornado forms on the south-western side of a thunderstorm, so you always want to put yourself just to the south or south-east.

When a storm rotates it's like when you pull a string around a top: whatever direction you pull the string, that's the direction the storm will veer off to. So you've always got to be watching. You never get yourself in a position where you don't have an escape. We take safety extremely seriously.

It's very different following a hurricane versus a tornado. With the tornado you want to stay out of the way; you don't want it to hit you. But with a hurricane, the whole idea is to get into the eye of it and you have to go through the worst of the hurricane to get there.

So what I do is: I'm watching the path of a hurricane and trying to figure out where the eye is going to make landfall. And then I go on Google Earth and look for structures, like multi-level, concrete parking garages or any place that has a fairly high elevation in case the water gets too deep from all the rain and storm surge. We try to find a place that we can gain elevation, to keep everybody safe, and then we park ourselves right there and let the thing come right atcha. When we did Hurricane Katrina, we had winds at our location – I have an anemometer that I always take with me – of over 170 miles per hour when the hurricane hit us, when the eye wall came across. We parked in a garage next to a hospital, which worked out really good because they had emergency power the whole time; I would give them weather data and they would let us come in and rest our bones on their couches.

And then when the eye wall came across, the winds were so fierce that the concrete structure shook and rattled so much that cracks started forming in the stairwells where we were standing. The whole idea is to get in the worst place that you could possibly get to and then let the eye come across. Once the eye goes across, then the southern eye wall hits you with winds from the opposite direction. You put yourself in harm's way with a hurricane, whereas with tornado chasing, you never want to be in harm's way. You want to stay out of the path of the tornado and watch it from a safe distance. It's definitely a lot different.

When Katrina made landfall we were actually on the north-north-western portion of the eye wall, so we had intense wind but we didn't get the water that they got further east. We were going to go to Diamondhead, Mississippi and then about three hours before I diverted us further west. It's a good thing, because the place that we were going to ended up 35 feet under water and was totally destroyed. So staying west and a little bit further inland was the right decision to make. It's OK to get into some water and it's OK to get into a lot of wind, but you don't want to risk your vehicle getting washed away or anything like that. So you have to be smart. Use a bit of common sense.

Oh, hurricanes are exciting, oh my gosh. We did Hurricane Ike that hit Galveston back in 2008. There's a hotel out on Galveston Island we stayed in that's about 30 feet above sea level and we watched the waves slam into the sea wall, shooting water 60–70 feet up in the air, with 100-mile-per-hour winds. It was pretty extreme. And then the next morning after the water receded, when the hurricane went inland, there were yachts sitting on the interstate highway and you had to drive around all these boats that were on the road.

But hurricanes are a blast. If you like *really* high adrenaline, it's insane. Because you get in a hurricane and the sensory input is just incredible. I mean, if you've never heard winds blowing 150 miles per hour, it sounds like a waterfall – the most giant, violent waterfall you could imagine right over the top of your head. And you hear the winds roaring through the trees and buildings, you hear glass breaking, things getting ripped, bricks falling and trees getting knocked down. It's just constant sensory input. The first time you do it, it scares the heck out of ya. Then after that it's not so bad.

We had a situation in North Dakota on 9 June 2001. We had a violent tornado across the road right in front of us and we got hit with the winds that wrap around the back of the supercell. They were blowing probably 110, 120 miles per hour. And this tornado spun right through a populated area. We waited for the wind to subside and then started driving and all of a sudden we see these houses down and there was a vehicle about 500 feet off the road in a ditch that had obviously been picked up by the tornado and thrown out there. It was crumpled up; mangled big time and I knew I had to stop and see if anybody was in it. We always keep first-aid kits in the vans if we come across a devastated area, we have the duty to humanity to stop and render assistance.

So I pulled off the highway and this guy's head raises up in the car and I run across the field yelling, 'Come on, come on! Get up! Come with us!' He climbs out the window and runs towards me and at that point I realise he's soaked in blood. From his shoulder blade diagonally all the way down to his right hip he was laid open all the way to the bone. He was losing a tremendous amount of blood and when he got in the van, he starts shaking and shivering and he's like, 'Oh, I thought I was going to die out there. I was just sure I was going to die. The tornado picked me up and threw me out in the field. I know I'm hurt. I just don't know how bad.' Then all of a sudden his eyes just rolled back in his head and he went into shock. We got him to the hospital and he survived.

I came across a situation many years ago in Sedalia, Missouri back in the early 2000s where a tornado had hit a trailer park. I started digging through rubble and I came across a woman that had been severed in two by a giant piece of sheet metal. You've got to be prepared for anything. It's not a nice thing to have happen but you've got to be prepared.

We had two bad times in 2011: one in Mississippi/Alabama and one in Missouri. Back on 27 April there was an absolute, horrendous tornado outbreak. Almost 400 people lost their lives that day. And the last one was a violent F5 tornado that went through the town of Turnerville and killed about 40 people en route. We came across this little town called Rose Hill that was absolutely devastated and started digging through the rubble, trying to help anybody that needed it. We spent a long time there trying to help where we could.

And then four weeks later a tornado hit the town of Joplin, Missouri that killed 180 people. We were actually chasing that storm and got trapped in the city trying to get out. We were coming down a road called Range Line Road and the tornado crossed as a violent F5; we were 30 seconds ahead of it. If we'd have had an obstacle preventing us from moving, I wouldn't be talking to you right now. Joplin was a very humbling experience; we were extremely close to being one of the fatalities ourselves. Just trying to get out of the way of this big, violent tornado was quite humbling.

Storms are going to happen whether we're there or not. I'm a ham radio operator, I'm CPR (cardiopulmonary resuscitation) and first-aid certified and if we come across some devastation, then we stop and help. We're reporting the whole time to the National Weather Service as we're out there seeing things. If you look at hurricanes, I would probably have to say Hurricane Katrina was the most humbling experience because we saw some of the devastation before we were able to get out of town.

On 16 June 2010 it was absolutely insane. All the other storm chasers were in Wyoming chasing this big low-pressure system that was coming out. We decided to take a gamble and play it way east into South Dakota where there was a lot of moisture, it was really humid and there was a lot of instability piling into a warm front to a boundary, and typically along a boundary you get a lot of wind shearing. We sat and watched the storm form by ourselves – nobody else around – in the middle of nowhere. That storm anchored itself to the warm front and dropped 22 tornados over a four-hour period, ranging from really weak F0s to violent F4s. You could almost sit out on a lawn chair with a cold beer in one hand and your camera in the other and watch. That storm just wasn't going anywhere.

Typically, most storms move along at a pretty good clip, maybe 30–40 miles per hour. But this storm just anchored itself right on that boundary and it spun and spun and spun and spun and spun. Sheer quantities of tornados… You know, I've been doing this for a long time and I'd never had a storm that dropped 22 tornados during its life cycle. And it didn't even move 10 miles. It just sat there and spun and dropped and spun and dropped. One time, we had twin tornados right to the north about a half a mile away and off to the west there was a big, violent, ¾-mile-wide tornado that was probably 2 miles away and then off to our south another skinny, little, elephant-trunk-shaped tornado formed and dropped down. So at one point in time, we had four tornados that encompassed 270 degrees. That was very exciting. That was intense.

Oh, it's crazy.

STORY TOLD BY ROGER

DANGER FACT:

At least 1,836 people died in Hurricane Katrina. The deadliest tornado in history was in Bangladesh in 1989 which killed approximately 1,300 people. The heaviest hailstones on record fell in Bangladesh, too, in April 1986; weighing over a kilogram, they are reported to have killed 92 people.

EXTREME FACT:

'Very large' hurricanes have a radius greater than 552 miles. The eye of a hurricane is typically 20–40 miles in diameter.

The most extreme tornado in recorded history was the Tri-State Tornado, which roared through Missouri, Illinois and Indiana on 18 March 1925. It holds records for longest path length (219 miles), longest duration (about 3.5 hours) and fastest forward speed (73 miles per hour). In addition, it is the deadliest single tornado in United States history (695 dead).

THE STUNT PERFORMER

Extreme rating: 💀💀💀💀💀
Danger level: ▁▁▁▪▪▪▪▪□□□
Criteria: Specialist technical skills; ideally acting experience
Skills: Physical fitness and dexterity; technical skills in relation to the specific type of work – such as car or fire stunts; courage; patience; acting; flare for dramatic effect; work ethic for potentially long hours in uncomfortable conditions; risk awareness, strategies and acceptance
Salary: £450 (US $700) per day up to six-figure salaries for top stunt performers

I had an accident as a stuntman and my memory went; I have big scars around my head. We were doing a car stunt in Denmark. I don't remember what happened. There was no pain but my head was split open in two places and I was unconscious for about an hour and a half. When I came round, there was a production girl holding my hand and I saw her wince so I realised something must have gone badly wrong. I'd driven through a building at 70 miles per hour and then off a pier into the water. I must have got knocked out in that building. It's supposed to be all made from balsa wood, but we think something in there got me and when I hit the water at 70 miles per hour I must have also hit the front of my head on the steering wheel or one of the instruments. I only had a lap belt on.

THE STUNT PERFORMER

My one fear was that if the car turned over, they wouldn't get me out, but the American special effects guy did a brilliant job. I was actually being pulled along on a wire, there's no engine in the car. He said he was pulling at a ratio of about 2:1 and he got up to 35 miles per hour. I looked at the distance and I thought, *that's 70–75 miles per hour, we'll never get to that speed by then*, but I think that was the shock – the speed that we took off – and that stopped me from getting my head down. I was supposed to get down going through the building, come up for the cameras and then get down again going into the water – those were my instructions but whether I went through that sequence I do not know. All I do know is that he saved my life. The car turned over and we had divers down there in the dark. This was two in the morning in the pitch black. Sixty-four stitches I had. An inch lower and I would have been in real trouble.

I'm a stuntman and a stunt coordinator; I've been doing it since 1965, man and boy. Sadly many of my friends are dead now, a couple through the job. You try to make it as safe as possible; but accidents do happen – as with me. There was an accident on *Harry Potter* recently and the boy's still in a wheelchair.

I am an ex-paratrooper and when I first started filming in '65, they were still making lots of war films and because I knew how to use a rifle, fire a gun, march and so on, it was a great advantage. I was in a group of ex-paras on *From Russia With Love* abseiling down the volcano. I've done nine Bond films.

I specialise in car stunts. I was a film extra for about three years and being an extra does teach you to work to the camera. It was very valuable experience. What happened is they did a Bond film called *Casino Royale* – the original one – and they wanted a girl to drive an E-type Jag quite quickly round a mountain road while being chased by David Niven in a Bentley, and they had a female racing driver for it. She was much quicker than me but hadn't worked to a camera before, so she would come through a bend and too quickly out the other side.

They eventually gave me a trial so I put gravel on the ground and got the arse going and the dust clouding up and the American director – with a cigar in his mouth – said 'Gaw, that's exactly what I want! You've got the job!' So that was the start of it; knowing how to work to camera and going for the dramatic effect. I was in and she was out, sadly. So I first doubled as a girl in a miniskirt for a James Bond film!

It was quite funny, because I had my own E-type – a 3.8 – at the time. I'm great pals with the director now but the producer then said, 'Look, can we borrow your car and pay for the damage?' So I said, 'Well, supposing it's beyond damage?' and he replied, 'Oh, it won't be, but we'll pay you £800 (US $1,250)' (which was the value of it then). So I said to the director, 'Do a good job of it,' and he put another charge of explosive in and the flames went 30 feet high! The car was a write-off. The producer bit through his cigar and said, 'I don't think we're going to be able to repair that!' With the money off that I bought my first house in Kensington.

I've done stuff for *The Bill, London's Burning, Dangerfield, Heartbeat,* Bond, *Star Wars, Sherlock Holmes*, *Robin Hood*… I did *The Sweeney* for years. And *The Professionals*. Eighty-two films and TV shows.

I used to race sports cars, Sprites, but they normally give me old bangers because I'm always turning them over or wrecking them! Old Fords or Jaguars. I've turned two or three Jaguars. I've done about forty altogether – including a police car off a transporter lorry.

There are three ways to turn a car. In the old days you just had a ramp – wooden, or metal if you were lucky – and you'd drive up there and have a 'kicker' maybe 2 or 3 feet from the end and that would kick you off. You turn the wheels the opposite way so it spins you in the right direction. There is now a pipe ramp which is a long steel pipe – the same principle with a kicker on the end. It's on a stand and you grease it up so the car slides quite well. Then there's a third way where they put a cannon in the car, you press a button, the cannon comes out and it flips over.

Inside the car you have a roll cage, padded up knees and elbows, and if you are lucky a crash helmet, depending on the shot. I have a small jockey helmet with a wig on top I use sometimes.

The long jumps are mainly done using sheer speed and sometimes a ramp. One of the longest ramps I used was jumping off Tower Bridge doubling as John Wayne in a Ford Capri. They had a big meeting about it and said to me: 'We don't particularly mind if you kill yourself but you are not jumping the bridge!' They were worried that I would damage it. So what they made me do in the film was reverse down to the bottom and they shot me coming up, then they closed the bridge and I drove it down the other side and dumped it into a skip. Then we put a ramp in between and I jumped the ramp so we had the shot of me in mid-air. They stuck it all together and it looks like I'm jumping the bridge. John Wayne said to me, 'Frank, next time we'll jump it'.

Peter – the other stuntman in a Jaguar – did jump it and got charged for it! He jumped with one side closed and the other open by 6–8 feet. There's a photograph of him with a fag hanging out of his mouth and a policeman writing down the charge in his little book. They dropped the case in the end.

It was more fun in those days. It's advanced tremendously now. I used to be on £10 (US $15) a day.

I had previously doubled John Wayne in *Brannigan* and he had a go at me on my first day. I had to drive a C-type at him and the director said to me, 'Come in like this' so I came in like he asked and Wayne said, 'That looked f***ing terrible'. So I said, 'Well, what do you want?' He said, 'I want you to come straight through there' – and I was doing 70 miles per hour. He slapped me afterwards on the shoulder and drawled, 'That wasn't bad, kid.'

I was once doubling John Thaw in a film and had to crash through a brick wall. They were actually wooden bricks but one of them came through the windscreen and I split my eye and had a couple of stitches. I have gone through a wall with real bricks but no cement and it was bloody dangerous. Luckily I threw myself under the windscreen. It was for a commercial and I was talking to an older stuntman who said, 'Frank, lean back in your seat' and thank God I never listened to him because the bricks would have landed on me. I just put a back pad on and went under the front.

I was getting ready on *Minder* for the first day of filming and George Cole had brought his wife and son in to see the car turn over. This taxi turned up and a lovely looking woman got out with this young boy and asked if George Cole was around. I didn't know him at the time so asked if he was one of the painters! I don't remember the turn over but I remember getting a bollocking!

The last big stunt I did was for health and safety. I played a tractor driver and had to turn it over. I had trouble with that. It was a film showing you what *not* to do on a steep hill in the mud. I had turned one over before in an earlier film by accident and the people paying for the tractor weren't happy but the director had loved it! So I thought I'd do it easily but I tried four or five times and couldn't get it over. We didn't have a ramp so I wandered around and found an old square cesspit and tried once more using that and it turned OK. It went with quite a bang because it was about 7 tonnes.

I've done a few motorbike and horse stunts and some falls. There was an interesting one in *Indiana Jones and the Temple of Doom* where I'm going down a cliff with Harrison Ford. I'd been with him on the *Star Wars* films so knew him quite well. We were 135 feet up and falling on a wire, fighting each other off a bridge. Harrison wanted to fight me and not the actor because he knew I'd get it right and not hit him! Because I got on well with Harrison I did several shots with him in *Indiana Jones* and *Star Wars*.

I worked on the very first *Star Wars* film and for three months on the third one, *Return of the Jedi*. I was Taym Dren-garen in *Return of the Jedi* fighting Luke Skywalker on the Khetanna ship over the Great Pit of Carkoon. Peter Diamond was in charge and he'd often say, 'Frank, get in that costume.' I was a Stormtrooper in *A New Hope* and an Endor Commando and the speeder biker in *Return of the Jedi*. I met Carrie Fisher (Princess Leia) on *Star Wars* – she used to love messing around. She's outrageous; a great, great character. We used to go out in the evenings together after filming.

The speeder biker scene in *Return of the Jedi* was done twice – once in the woods and once in front of a blue screen with Carrie Fisher. In the studio, I'm on a motorbike, stationary and trapped in a 4 x 2-inch block, with a camera over the way. George Lucas is shouting, 'Frank, you're going two hundred miles per hour through the trees!' I'm looking at the camera, in front of a blue screen, but George would see the whole scene. George then was full of energy and enthusiasm. It wasn't a big money film. We didn't know it was going to be so huge. We'd recorded up in the giant redwood forest near San Francisco. Ten days with Carrie playing a Stormtrooper on a bike. It was a fantastic time.

I didn't find the Stormtrooper suit too difficult. I know a couple of stuntmen walked off because they found it claustrophobic. I never found it, to be honest. I've certainly done films which were more claustrophobic and worrying. I don't remember being hot in the costumes, in fact up in the Redwood trees it was actually cold; I used to walk up to the road out of the shade to warm up.

The Ewoks were lovely. Great fun and outrageous.

Richard Burton shot me in *Where Eagles Dare*. I was the radio operator. On my call sheet it says: Clint Eastwood, Frank and Richard Burton and

I'm thinking: which one never made it?! But it's great. I enjoy the time on set and being part of the industry. You learn special tricks like turning cars over. It's been a good life really.

STORY TOLD BY FRANK

Eddie Kidd, Evel Knieval, Houdini and Jackie Chan have all been stunt performers. Evel Knieval broke 433 bones during his career, earning him an entry in Guinness World Records as the survivor of 'most bones broken in a lifetime'. Jackie Chan fractured his skull, dislocated his pelvis and broke his fingers, toes, nose, both cheekbones, hips, sternum, neck, ankle and ribs.

Eddie Kidd's most famous motorcycle stunt was jumping 120 feet at 90 miles per hour. In *The Great Escape*, Bud Ekins, pursued by Germans, jumped his motorcycle 60 feet over a barbed-wire fence.

In *Conan the Barbarian* Corrie Jansen leaped 182 feet off a cliff, a record freefall for a woman.

In *Live and Let Die* Ross Kananga as James Bond used four crocodiles as stepping stones to reach safety on the other side. Kananga, who owned the crocodile farm, did the stunt five times. During the fourth attempt, the last crocodile bit through the shoe and into his foot.

THE UNDERCOVER COP

Extreme rating: ☠☠☠☠☠
Danger level: ▁▁▄▄▮▮▮▮▯
Criteria: Experience in a police role, but not mandatory; right 'fit' of character and look; pass the assessment stage and psychometric tests
Skills: Emotional intelligence; psychological stability; acting and creative skills; excellent memory; calm under pressure; quick thinking; integrity
Salary: Same as a police officer – £32,610 (US $50,780) after two years' probation

I work for a department called SO10 which is a specialist covert operations unit for the Metropolitan Police. There are two tiers of undercover work: Test Purchase, which is low level £10–£20 (US $15–30) crimes on the street, and Tier One, which is long-term, deep infiltration using 'legends'.

A legend is an identity and a complete life you build for yourself; one that you can fall back on and people can reference. It involves companies, girlfriends, birth certificates, passports, bank accounts… so if somebody were to look into your life all those bits of bio data would stand up to the attention test.

What you do is build several legends. For example, if you use the name Tony, you could be Anthony, Tony, Tone, or Ant for example. The Anthony legend might work best with my particular forte which was money laundering, fine art and jewellery. I could draw on a top level legend like Anthony if I was working on a money-laundering job, pitch up in a blazer and a pink shirt and play posh. But then you can also play different ends of the market. So you can do your criminal end as Tone.

For example, somebody stole a £180,000 (US $280,000) brooch in an aggravated burglary with a shotgun and he had it for sale. We knew that it was stolen and knew where it was stolen from, so my role was to draw out the brooch, identify it and pretend to place it in the market. But I couldn't play that as Anthony in the blazer and pink shirt so I went down to meet him as Tony in a leather jacket and wearing a couple of sovereign rings.

So that's the spread of the legends.

To get a job in undercover they identify you early on. You don't want too many blokes with broken noses being geezers, so they spot you. They generally want people with a little bit of experience, but that's not always the case. There are some very talented individuals who do it who have very limited experience with the police but are very good at what they do. They may go in long term and do it for the entire length of their police career. And they'll do deep, deep work – they'll go away for years.

I thought I would come in as a buyer. I'd done drug work but they wanted me to fill a niche on the financial side. So I got a diploma in gemmology – in precious stones – and trained in valuing and breaking polished and rough diamonds. If, for instance, someone gave me some cash, I would say to them that I could place it in a very moveable, tangible product – as in diamonds. They are very easy to move around the world and then realise at the other end where you get a cheque, so that's how you 'wash' the money.

In training you do a variety of psychometric tests, a number of interviews and you go and see the shrink. They make an assessment of you and then you go forward to do the initial course. You go into role (none of it is classroom based) and play out live simulations working around the country, staying in hotels, driving various cars, getting phone calls, suffering from sleep deprivation, getting briefings from senior officers and so on. You play three or four roles over a month, up against other undercover police officers and with police surveillance teams following you around – it's good practice for them too.

At the end of that they completely debrief your performance from start to finish. It's quite an interesting debrief; very personal and frank. So it's not really for the fragile or emotional.

One of the most difficult things is Stockholm syndrome. The name comes from a bank robbery in Stockholm where the victims were held for several days. When the police eventually raided and said point out the hostage takers, they wouldn't. They had become like-minded and sympathetic. So you have to go and see the shrink every three months and they sign you off, to say whether you are sane or not. The boys who do the paedophile work go and see the shrink once a month because of the nature of the work.

And so much of the work is on your own. It's very solitary. There might be situations where you're deployed for three or four months living in a pretty horrible part of the country with only four or five meetings happening.

There are a number of different ways you can approach a job. We do a lot of cold infiltration which is long-term work. It wouldn't be unusual in a longer term operation for us to take a house or a flat beside the target. Cold infiltration – in pubs or wherever it might be – is difficult. You can imagine, the individuals we are up against are very in tune with tactics and techniques and everything else. However, most undercover work starts with an informant's information, so it's warm. You get introduced by the informant and then you distance yourself away. I've done jobs where I've been eleventh or twelfth man in.

There are a lot of long-term jobs. Some jobs have run on for years and will continue to run because it's all very subtle.

There are only a few long-term Tier One operators in the UK, so it gets interesting when you're doing more than one job. It wouldn't be unusual for me to carry four or five phones and each phone would be a different job. I used to write something on the back of them so if one rang, I knew right away which job it was.

So there's a lot of thought and angles, a web of information.

It's not always what they call 'buy and bust' – you know, buy some drugs, buy some guns… there are some very unusual cases. There was the guy who killed ****** and I got briefed up for a 'cell infiltration'. He'd been brought up on a TDA (taking and driving away) and although he was a suspect in the murder investigation we didn't have forensic evidence at that stage so he was going to be released. They wanted me to go into cell infiltration and befriend him. I would play the role of a property developer and, as he was a builder, I'd ask him to do some property development for me when we both got out. We'd give him a van we could trace and know his living address and that way we would have control over him.

Getting control somehow is important. The whole thing is to try and create an environment where we have control. You can imagine some of these individuals are headstrong, violent people. We had one particular guy we were trying to buy some guns off. He held his girlfriend's mother and father hostage and pulled their finger- and toenails out with pliers, so you sit down with this individual and you know he's an incredibly violent man.

So the danger side of things is quite interesting.

It basically comes down to 1) whether they like you – because that's key; and 2) whether you are 'attractive' enough – whether they feel they can do business with you. The whole motivation is about making money, so you are either introducing something to them where they could make money or you are buying things from them.

The way an undercover trade works is usually there is a commodity that I'm looking to buy so I demonstrate that I've got the cash, I flash the cash. The moment you flash the cash, greed takes a hold, once they see something's tangible. That's why we're keen to get the cash out as quickly as we can.

Then they bring on the product – the painting, the drugs, the guns – and want to do the swap, but it never gets to that because we always hit them with an arrest. That's the mechanics in the way that the deal is done.

In America what the FBI do is they mirror their suspects and try to meet like for like, trying to match character types and backgrounds. Over here we do less of that because England's a small place with a pub culture and it's all about who you know and how you know them. So you come in at a different angle. The money man's always quite interesting, which I used to play a lot of. I would come in at an angle that was a bit aloof – it works as reverse psychology. 'I don't want to deal with you.' It not only makes them want it more, but with that superiority over them you don't need to get down to an East End pub and enter into their chat and answer all their questions.

But a lot of the lads who do the more gritty work, the long-term infiltration in the council estates for drugs, murders, guns or whatever it might be, they do meet like for like and they have a seriously tough time, much tougher than me; they're much better at that than me.

Most of it's about sitting down and being convincing with the individual. I've sat down with some targets and they've said 'I can smell the old bill from a mile away' and then they talk to you not knowing that you are in fact an undercover police officer.

But usually they're very in tune. Criminals will always debrief every single arrest or operation in great detail.

I went for a meal in a restaurant near a suspect's shop and two surveillance walked in, following him. And he said, 'They're surveillance officers – are they with you?' I said, 'No – I don't know what you're talking about.' And he said, 'I've got my suspicions that you are an undercover police officer.' So I said, 'Let's call the deal off then,' calling his bluff. That was a big shout. But he knew. I still think to this day he knew.

The difference is, you see, when they get up in the morning, their whole mind is concentrated on not going to prison. They know at some stage – because of what they do – that they will be followed, their phone or car's going to be bugged, they're going to be turned in by an informant or caught out by an undercover police officer.

A lot of criminals will just walk away if they don't like you, but I've been in situations where someone will pick you up and say, 'I'll take you to my flat and we'll have a chat there.' However, we're wearing recording equipment and if you get rumbled, they might not let you go; you're not in control any more.

One of the biggest ruses villains will use if they're any good is say: 'I love everything you're talking about, fantastic; I haven't done anything wrong myself but I'll introduce you to a couple of people who might be able to help you. By the way, let's have a chat in a certain town in Europe.' Now we can't get authority to meet people in some countries – their legal system doesn't allow undercover police officers. You've got to be able to see your accuser – their real identity. So of course what they do is turn round and say, 'Come to X town.' And we can't go. So there are these little tests. You don't ever go off the rule book. You have to be very careful. Because fundamentally the whole reason you're doing it is to build an evidential package. So you can stand up in court.

That's the other thing – courts – you give evidence behind a screen, sometimes you give evidence with voice distortion. I've done accents as well.

There's a lot of creativity, I suppose.

A lot of the drugs work – ecstasy, pills and so on – I did with the legend of working in the City – 'My city mates want some coke'. I couldn't go along and buy heroin, like some of the other boys and girls could, because of my profile and character. But I did have some success with the coke aspect. So I might go along and say, 'Give me an ounce,' because you always buy a small amount first, and then turn round and say, 'Look, let me buy half a kilo,' and that would pretty much be my bit before I brought the big boys in. I'd then say, 'Actually, I've got some friends of mine who would be very interested in more.'

There are all sorts of different jobs. For example when we caught *****. The way we caught this well-known London criminal was with two girls – very good girls off the undercover books – who went in knowing that he was going to be drinking in a certain wine bar. They walk in and say, 'Oh, you're *****! Can I buy you a drink?' And then they invite him to a party at the Docklands. Unbeknown to *****, the entire party was an undercover party, completely staged. So there have been some massive coups.

By the way, there's no dispensation for drunk driving. But you have to be very convincing – to be brutally honest you go on the piss with them. In America you aren't allowed to, they say you can't induce a statement from a suspect if you've had alcohol, but over here some of the best confessions we've had are over 20 pints!

You get a lot of support from other undercover people. There's an index – like an actors' book. You may say: 'I need a black guy, six foot, looks a bit heavy, and a blonde girlfriend who works for British Airways as a hostess,' (that's the reason she's away all the time) and so on. We also use a lot of foreigners; we train the Lithuanians, Portuguese, Swedish, Russians, Norwegians… and so if I needed some heavies – 'street furniture' we call them – we'd contact the book and get two Russians or Lithuanians.

You script a job.

When it comes to the work of the female undercover officers, it's fascinating within the criminal fraternity how influential the girlfriends, wives and mums are. They have massive power. So sometimes the infiltration is done female to female. And that works brilliantly. I may go in as the son of a woman and she'd do all the negotiations, explaining that her husband was in prison. We've had some real successes where women have done the negotiating.

The difficulty when you come into a role is your ego. We've got lots of guys and girls who have done it for a long time and it's quite interesting when you've got some very experienced boys out. Because they're playing benign roles – door openers, drivers, bouncers – but they're very intelligent, very capable people.

You end up maybe working with two or three you know really well, and of course, the more you work with them, the more the legends overlap. You can actually use real jobs as references. So the legends themselves can end up creating their own histories which intertwine.

There's nothing better and more exhilarating than sitting down with an individual and them not knowing what and who you are. It does feed the ego but then you need to keep control of that.

You get a buzz out of it.

You yearn for the phone call to go and play.

STORY TOLD BY * * * * *

The stress in undercover work may result in drug or alcohol abuse in some agents. They are more prone to the development of an addiction as they suffer greater stress, they are isolated and often drugs or alcohol are very accessible and part of the job.

Since World War Two, one of the longest and most expensive covert operations was the CIA's 'Operation Cyclone' which ran for ten years and cost reputedly hundreds of millions of dollars per year.

THE VOLCANOLOGIST

Extreme rating: ☠☠☠☠☠
Danger level: ▁▁◢◢■■□□□□
Criteria: Geochemistry; geophysics; geology
Skills: Physical ability to do fieldwork in remote and hostile environments including descending to the seabed in submersibles; curiosity; passion for knowledge; patience and rigour to apply for funding
Salary: Research funded

I live in Iceland and I study volcanoes. I was very lucky to be born here.

For geologists, Iceland is like paradise – our volcanoes are very active. It's a wonderful geological laboratory. This is where I became hooked when I was a kid.

Volcanoes are very important for us in many ways. They are, of course, a natural hazard but they are also a source of energy. In Iceland the heat from volcanoes – the geothermal energy – heats almost all homes and generates electric power. Of course, volcanoes are just the surface manifestation of heat deep inside the Earth. So ultimately, I'm really more interested in deeper features, the sources of the energy, the forces that create and drive volcanoes.

What I do is many different things. I do basic geologic mapping. You go out in a volcanic area, you study the rocks, you determine what the

179

distribution of the different rock types is, you find the surface and you use that information to construct an image or a concept of the volcano and how it works. So the information you get from geologic mapping is very important in creating a hazard map. A hazard map gives you an idea of what types of hazards are associated with a volcano and what the distribution is.

We work in collaboration with regional or national governments and provide to them hazard maps or other information about the volcano. And sometimes they take note of it, sometimes they don't, because there are many issues… So in many cases, disaster or tragedy is waiting to happen.

I work in volcanoes all over the world. I worked a lot in Indonesia. Lately I've been working in Papua New Guinea which is a very exciting volcanic area. I work, of course, in Iceland, where I am now. In Italy, Greece, the Mediterranean, Central and South America, Galapagos, the West Indies, all over the world. There are volcanoes in very many parts of the world, except none in Britain. There were in Britain about 15 million years ago.

I don't have a favourite volcano. It's like your children: you're not supposed to pick favourites.

So it means a lot of outdoor activity, which is the main part of what I enjoy about it; the ability to make a living by working outdoors and studying the Earth. It's a never-ending search for information. It's always exciting. You go into a new gully or climb a mountain that you haven't been on – all these findings are new. It's so exciting, just to know what's around the corner and get more information. And you are the first one to find it out. So it's like a treasure hunt for information. It's been more than 40 years that I've been doing this work and I do it all the time. It's my passion.

A lot of the science I do is called geochemistry, 'chemistry of the rocks'. So you collect the rocks and in order to get more information out of them, you chemically analyse them, in particular, chemically analyse the minerals that are in the rocks. And so that is the basic research process. But the most time-consuming aspect is still the fieldwork, the outdoors activity.

Most of the time, I'm just collecting samples at the surface, but in some cases, we drill maybe 0.6–1.2 miles down; in one case we actually descend into the Earth. There's a crater in Iceland where you can descend 490 feet down, into the conduit of a volcano. You go down vertically through the crater, through a 6.5-foot-wide pipe, down into a chamber. It's unique; there's no place on the Earth like it.

Whatever it takes, I do. I study submarine volcanoes a lot. I've spent time in research submarines; going down to the bottom of the sea 3,280 feet is part of the job – not one I enjoy, but somebody has to do it.

I've been in two- to four-person submersibles. They carry an oxygen supply and there's a pilot and the scientists. They are self-propelled; they don't have a tether to a ship, they are just free. In one case I was on a submarine volcano in the Caribbean called 'Kick 'em Jenny' and we went down to 2,300 feet just touching the sea floor and then we lost all power, lights, everything. We were sitting in total darkness for an hour and the pilot couldn't get anything going. We had oxygen, but when you exhale, you exhale carbon dioxide and the carbon dioxide was building up in the capsule because without power you can't strip the air of CO_2. We were getting dizzy and finally managed to release a small balloon that helped to lift the submersible and bring it back to the surface. So that was a very unpleasant experience. That could have been the end there.

There are more volcanoes on the sea floor than there are on land because the area is bigger. There's more activity; so you can see underwater eruptions, hot springs and you can study the geology of the sea floor just like you study it on land. There are mountains and canyons and all sorts of features that are interesting to explore. Magma comes out the same way but it behaves a little differently because of the cooling effect of the water; it produces lava flows called 'pillow lava'. There are still explosive eruptions and hot springs, geysers, geothermal activity… just like on the surface.

I visit both dormant and active areas. I visit active volcanoes and participate in research on ongoing eruptions and I also study the deposits from past eruptions. I am interested in the biggest eruptions that have taken place on the Earth and I reconstruct them, just like the detective goes to the crime scene and looks for clues. I go to the site of the volcano that has erupted maybe 10,000 years ago and I find the deposit that it created. And from the character and nature of the deposit I can tell you what happened, a blow-by-blow account of the actual volcanic activity, from the nature of the layers or the deposits. And so a lot of my work is really related to study of ancient eruptions by the clues they leave on the ground.

Usually, if we know what the volcano has done in the past, we know what it is capable of in the future.

We measure the size of the eruption by two things: one is the amount of material that is produced and we measure that in cubic kilometres of magma. A cubic kilometre is a lot of stuff, as you can imagine, and we have eruptions that range from one tenth of a cubic kilometre to eruptions that are over 1,000 cubic kilometres [240 cubic miles]; it's a tremendous range in the size of eruptions. So that is the most fundamental measure of an eruption: the volume erupted in cubic kilometres. And the second thing we measure is the rate of eruption: how many kilograms per second are coming out of the volcano. That is a very important thing. That's like when you turn your tap on in your house – is it just dripping out or is it blasting out at full force? We can measure both of these things by doing fieldwork on the volcano. Even for eruptions that took place thousands of years ago, we can get that type of information from study of the deposits.

THE VOLCANOLOGIST

Vesuvius and Krakatoa are amongst the most famous volcanoes, but not for volume or eruption size. Vesuvius is about 1.4 cubic miles and Krakatoa about 4.3 cubic miles. I've worked a lot on the eruption of Tambora in Indonesia. In 1815, that produced 24 cubic miles. So that's a big eruption and it had a global impact. It killed 117,000 people. Another big eruption that I worked on is Santorini in the Aegean. That occurred in the Bronze Age and that was about 14.3 cubic miles. So these are not as well known, but they are much bigger and much more important events. Vesuvius and Krakatoa are well known, but smaller.

Yellowstone is an active volcano. There's no indication that it is about to erupt, but it's an active volcano and it will erupt in the future. We don't know whether it will be a large monster eruption or a relatively small one. All we know is that there is a lot of magma in the reservoir beneath the surface.

Many active volcanoes are in Indonesia. There are about 150 active volcanoes in Indonesia and there's an eruption there somewhere every day. Many parts of the Earth are, and will continue to be, volcanically active. So I'll always have a job.

Sometimes I'm away for maybe two months. Usually a big expedition is two months because it takes a lot of effort to set it up and bring all the equipment, all the people. And sometimes I work with ships because I do a lot of work on submarine volcanoes. I once worked with a ship with a crew of 100 people on it. We were drilling into the sea floor, many little cavities in the Caribbean. Sometimes I work alone. Sometimes in submersibles or submarines. So it just depends on what tools you require to do the job. In the past, I've taken graduate students on my expeditions; that's part of their training and education.

My training is in geology, geochemistry and some geophysics. You have to have a passion for knowledge. Just like in any field of science, you have to have a very strong, innate curiosity; an interest and enthusiasm for it. You have to want to do the work, to create the enthusiasm you require to live in difficult situations and to push on when times are tough: both in terms of getting funding, which can be very tough, but also physically, to go out for the information. You need physical ability to live in the outdoors and to be willing to rough it. You're in situations that range from the tropics to the Arctic and from the ocean to the mountains.

There's always something new. In Indonesia, for example, I've been in a volcano called Ijen, East Java. It's a very big volcano with a big crater and there's a hot lake on the crater floor. On the sides of the lake there are fumaroles where massive sulphur deposits are being created. About three or four hundred people are mining in those terrible conditions, excavating the hot sulphur at 200–300°C and carrying it up on their shoulders out of the volcano. It's like a scene from Dante's *Inferno* or from hell. It's one of the most unforgettable sights I've seen on any volcano: the interaction of human activity and the volcanic energy. It's one that really sticks in my mind.

A live volcanologist is a good volcanologist! I've been doing it for 40 years and I've seen a lot of dangerous situations. I've never lost anybody who's been with me but I know five people who have been killed in volcanoes… friends. So it's a dangerous situation that you sometimes are presented with, because of the volcano or because of the environment that you're working in. Working in a submersible is dangerous. And I do quite a bit of scuba diving as well. That's dangerous. You can come close to dying of thirst in some volcanoes. Fallout from the volcanoes during explosions or pyroclastic flows – those are the deadliest aspects of volcanoes. So you see death, you come close to it. And I've been working in areas where, like in Colombia 1985, I came into an area where 22,000 people had been killed two days before in an eruption. You get into tragic situations.

THE VOLCANOLOGIST

I've got close to pyroclastic flows. You get very anxious, of course, because you have to judge, 'How big is it going to be? Am I going to be overwhelmed or am I OK where I am?' It's like watching a train go by but it doesn't have to stay on the rails. I've done that in a volcano called La Soufrière in St Vincent in the West Indies. It erupted in 1979 and we saw pyroclastic flows at close-range – 328 feet away. So that's scary. There's a lot of dust, but the heat isn't so bad. The heat from lava flows is much greater. With lava flows you can be 32 feet away, but the radiating heat is so great that you have to move away.

The best aspect is the potential of making a discovery. Every time you pick up a rock and look underneath it, or enter into a valley that has never been explored, you always have this sense that you are on the brink of making a discovery. And that is very exciting. That's what drives you, because maybe nobody has gotten to it or seen it before; you're there and now's your chance…

STORY TOLD BY HARALDUR

 **DANGER FACT:**

Volcanic activity can be dangerous in various ways: lava flows, pyroclastic flows, mud slides, landslides and the aftermath of ash and dust. This does not include earthquakes and tsunamis caused by volcanic activity.

Between 1975 and 2000, 86 per cent of people killed by direct volcanic activity died in Colombia on 13 November 1985 – almost 22,000 deaths were recorded there. Most of these people died in Armero due to mud flows.

(Data from the United Nations Environment Programme 2005)

EXTREME FACT:

There are about 500 active volcanoes in the world today – most of them along the Pacific 'Ring of Fire'. About 50 of these erupt each year. The United States is home to 50 active volcanoes including the 'super volcano' in Yellowstone National Park. Approximately 500 million people live near active volcanoes.

THE WORLD SUPERBIKE CHAMPION

Extreme rating: ☠☠☠☠☠
Danger level: ▁▁▃▄▅██▆□□
Criteria: Qualifying races
Skills: Natural talent for motorbike riding and racing; quick reactions; courage; confidence
Salary: From £105,000 (US $163,500) for a rookie to one well-known world champion earning an alleged £21 million (US $32.7 million) in one year

My stepdad bought me an 80-cc trials bike for Christmas when I was nine. I'd been seriously learning to play the piano for which I used to get quite a bit of stick, with my little leather satchel, glasses and braces. Then, when I got a motorbike for Christmas, it was much cooler than the piano playing; I instantly found I had 20 new mates. Everybody thought I was cool all of a sudden.

My mum hated it. But at that point my maximum speed was about 30 miles per hour so there wasn't too much danger to it. Little did she know that I'd be riding 200-plus miles per hour ten years later.

I'm from an old mining village and when the mine shut down I practised on all the slag heaps from the pits. We did a lot of competitions as well; four years of trials. I was quite talented as a trials rider but then saw motocross on TV and thought that was cool because it was fast and racing, so I tried my hand at that. But I was really short as a kid (I was twelve years old then) and riding a 125-cc – well, it was riding me rather than me riding it! My bravery was outdoing my talent; I didn't feel safe and I had a few crashes. Then I noticed road racing where the riders were all built like jockeys. I remember just falling in love with the discipline, thinking, 'This is for me. This is great. You don't have to get dirty; you don't have to clean your bike every time.'

Honestly, I've never liked getting my hands dirty. With motocross you get absolutely sludged up to the eyeballs; you can't see because you get that much crap in your eyes. My mum was complaining – she had to clean all the gear and we used to go down the jet-wash, clean the bike and then I had to stand there in my boots with mum jet-washing me down. So that was a big thing when I was younger because I hated cleaning the bike and as a child I never liked anything dirty; even now I hate it on my hands. And then there was the height. On the motocross bike I felt like the bike was just pulling me around, but in road racing all of a sudden I felt in control; I felt like I was able to push the bike to its limits.

My first bike was a Cagiva 80 – an Italian bike – and in my first race I finished fourth. I was a bit nervous but more of an excitable nervousness than a dreading nervousness. I was only 14. Luckily I found something that I just *did* and I was good at. With piano playing, I had to try hard because it didn't come easy. But with this I just jumped on a motorbike and I was fast. So that was the appeal as well, because you know a 14-year-old: anything that comes easy is great. And it did, it just came very easy to me; I was very comfortable. With no effort or much practice I was in the top three all of a sudden; I knew I'd found something I could enjoy. I was very competitive. And then with a bit of practice, the opportunities came to move up the ranks. I won that championship in my very first year. I was British Junior Champion. Nobody had heard of me because I'd come from a small mining village with no racing background and no racing family.

I went from getting lapped in that year on the Cagiva to riding a Honda CB500 and qualifying two seconds faster than second place in my first race. For sure, it was a fire that had lit inside me. Because of my personality – my personal background – my determination and hunger made racing ideal for getting rid of built-up frustrations. It was perfect for me.

I was with Honda for four years. On the CB500, I won every race but one. And because I was doing so well, halfway through that year Honda put me on a 600. This is at men's level; I was only sixteen. They had to change the rules for me, to 16 instead of 18, and I won the last five out of the eight races.

This was racing against the best in the UK. I mean at 16 I just jumped on a bike and rode it like I'd stolen it. And it just worked with what was going through my head and heart. I remember one race on a 1,000-cc bike that had 200 bhp (brake horsepower). At 16, I jumped on the bike in a one-off race and beat the guy that had won the championship that year. Something clicked in my head to give me the right mentality to do it.

At the end of '97, the bosses of Honda came to my mum's house and said to me: 'We want to take you to the world championship. We're going to enter you just to see.' And I was leading until the last lap, when the second-place guy overtook me. Which I thought was quite rude on the last lap!

And that's when everybody thought, 'He's leading the world already in one race.' It was just a natural transition. Something lit and I was away.

I didn't realise how good I was… I just jumped on; I wasn't doing anything special in my eyes. I remember first racing 600s, I qualified on the front row and I was battling for the lead when I fell off trying to overtake for first place. When I came back in, the Honda boss was a bit pissed off at me. He said, 'What happened?' I said, 'They were too slow, they were getting in my way.' He just looked at me and smiled. But when you're 16, it was completely the truth. To think that the best in the UK were 'too slow' and I felt they were holding me up! He still laughs about that.

But natural talent only gets you so far and then you have to really learn the race craft and try different techniques to improve. Because what happens with natural talent, as I've found, is you don't need to concentrate on what you're doing; it's completely unconscious. But if all of a sudden that natural talent is not getting the results, you need to find out how to improve. So the earlier you can do that, the better it is for you in your later career. In my first two years I was just fast and crashed quite a bit. I missed the mentoring.

I taught myself as much as I could. I was so into it; I used to watch TV and look at the body position and watch how they knee over to the floor and how some riders put their fingers on the clutch and the brake lever for different reasons. I looked at all these things to learn. You have to when you're young, because you go to all these exotic new tracks around the world racing against people who have ridden them for years. At championship level, the tracks are so narrow and undulating that anybody with a bit of bravery can stick their neck out and do quite well instantly. But then you go to the bigger tracks, the wider tracks, where there are more options for you to make differences as a rider, as a skilful rider... and at world championship level, they're all good. You've not got four people to beat, you've got 14. So these were the differences that I was learning when I went up the ladder. From 1997 I didn't win anything until 2003 when I joined world championship level racing. And I was doing OK; I was climbing the ladder, but...

There's so much you can learn. Even as a professional, there's so much you can learn. From adapting the braking technique, to using the rear brake in the right areas, to your body position on the bike. They go so fast now and you brake so late. When you brake, all the rear wants to do is lift off the floor, so you have to make sure your body is right back on the bike to balance it out – all these things that you have to think about at high speed. You can't be completely at one, and fast, until you can do it all unconsciously.

In World Superbikes you do knock-out heats like in Formula One, but you have to really jam the first one in on qualifying tyres and stick your neck out. You haven't got as much grip (because you're on quali tyres) and you've got to put in a really good time. Thursday's when we do a lot of press stuff. The paddock's open to the public for autographs and meeting the riders. And then out on Friday morning for an hour, Friday afternoon for another hour, and in-between the two sessions you'll be adjusting the bike; trying to get the optimum set-up. Then a quiet night Friday night, a bite to eat in hospitality and in bed for 10.30 p.m. And then up again on Saturday morning.

Friday afternoon and Saturday morning are the qualifying sessions for the shoot-out. It can work against you sometimes: if you've had a problem on Friday and then you wake up Saturday morning and it's raining… you're out. There are always these variables. It's amazing how many things have to go right. In a whole year, from February to October, all these variables have to go pretty much perfectly to become a champion. I mean you can do very well in seasons when you are talented and have a winning team, but to win a championship it's amazing how all these things have to come together – unbelievable.

On Saturday night, you are either laying in bed thinking, 'I'm in the hunt tomorrow' or 'I'm going to have to stick my neck out tomorrow, because not everything's worked out great for me.' All these different emotions. If there's been a real mismatch with the weather, like rain-dry-rain-dry; there are some scenarios where the conditions you're racing in haven't been the conditions you've done the whole weekend in. It can rain Friday and Saturday, then you may wake up Sunday morning and it's dry. Then it's a gamble. You go back to settings you know from before and hope for the best. But that's the same for everyone.

I never minded riding in the rain but when it's cold and raining your hands and knees go numb. Terrible. Can't get the feeling. When I crashed in 2005 – and it could only have happened in England – I broke the water pipe off the radiator and all the water drained from the engine. This was on Lap 1. I got back on and I didn't see it, riding around, but the team saw it on TV and they were just going to do a few laps before pulling me in. But I was going for the championship and needed the points. I finished the whole race. It was that cold and wet in England, that the air and water from the rain cooled the bike. Honda stripped the engine afterwards and they couldn't believe it; how little was damaged. Amazing. And the points from that race got me the championship.

Riding a machine and trying to get it to do what you want it to do, it's incredible how many people have to work on it. There are 30 guys on the team. Everybody from the engineer who knows exactly how everything's ticking on that thing, to the chef who will cook the right food to keep the body going – physically letting you do it. Like racing in Malaysia when it's 38°C, 60 per cent humidity: the need for fitness, nutrition and fluids means that all of a sudden the chef and the nutritionist are just as important as your suspension guy.

Each year the bikes get faster and faster and more and more powerful. And the thing with a motorcycle is, because of the pendulum effect and the fact they are rear-wheel driven, all the bike wants to do when you open the throttle is step up and go in a straight line. Naturally, with the physics of it, that's what it wants to do. So the more power you put in it, the more it wants to go straight, and the more physical it is for us to manipulate the bike to get it to where we want it to go. And that's why the faster tracks are so much harder work than the slower ones. When you're going really fast, the bike wants to go straight and you've got to really manhandle it. The faster tracks are always more physical when you're going from corner to corner in full. The slower tracks are always off the throttle, trying to get it to turn all the time.

It's amazing how much of it is a whole-body workout. You're going from side to side, off the bike, squatting on the foot-pegs, lifting your bum. You don't realise how many times in one race. You're on the throttle and you've got to keep yourself forward to stop the front wheel coming up. So there's a lot of pulling and then a lot of pushing, especially when you're braking. We're pulling a few g on the brakes and then g on the corners but because I've only got two wheels, you don't feel it so much. On the GP bikes we had carbon brakes – less weight than a Superbike – and just to give you an idea, at 200 miles per hour the MotoGP bike brakes 82 feet later at the same speed.

I went to Ducati after Honda. And then I crashed a little, I was a bit inconsistent, so I came back to the UK. But I went to Superbikes instead of the 600s so I moved up into international championships. I was doing quite well but then I had a crash at Cadwell Park in August 2000 and smashed my femur in three places. When I landed, my leg was wrapped around my head. As it was a test day, there were no ambulances at the track and so it took 45 minutes for one to come. I was lying on the floor like that for 45 minutes. I'd never seen my leg around there before!

So that was a big trauma. And because I did it in August I missed the last part of the season. But then luckily I met my manager, Roger, and he needed a cheap young rider, to team up with Neil Hodgson. I was spannered really; I was still on crutches when I met him. And he said, 'I'm going to get you a job with Neil Hodgson for two years in World Superbikes with Ducati.' And I thought he was off his head. I'd just come out of hospital with the most serious injury I'd ever had and someone was offering me the job of my dreams.

And that's where my Superbike career started. I'd come from having a really serious injury, worried that I'd not ride again, to having another opportunity.

Neil Hodgson was a British lad, so we could communicate really easily. And I was coming from quite low down, so I was no threat to him at that point. He still jokes now, 'I taught him too well.' He used to say: 'Try this. Try that.' Because the Ducati's a twin cylinder, compared to the four-cylinder bikes I'd ridden, the engine character is very different and the way to ride them is different. He taught me the differences in how to ride the bike, and the team was amazing. My engineer and the team manager had meetings Friday and Saturday nights looking at the telemetry of both bikes.

The engineer worked for both of us. He used to sit us down, Neil and me, and say: 'Neil's braking fifteen feet later than you. He's got a little bit less corner speed, so you're quicker in the middle, but look how he can get out the exit quicker.' Fifteen feet, that speed... amazing. *Blink*. It was all written out in plain English for me to go out there the next day and try it. And without any more effort, the lap times were coming down and that was specifically about how to ride a Superbike. Because anybody can ride a motorbike. With my natural talent, I could ride a motorbike. But with the amount of power that they've got now, you have to ride them in a certain way to get a good lap time. It wasn't all about just riding it like you'd stolen it. It was a skill. Like how to ride the corners.

So all this was a big learning curve. Three years with that team were good value in teaching me how to be a Superbike rider. I was with Ducati for five years, went on to the official Ducati team and won the championship in the first year. I'd gone from thirteenth in the 2001 championship to being world champion in 2004. From thirteenth, to seventh, to third, to first.

If I had not had the guidance and help from my manager and the teams and people I was working for, all I'd have done is injured myself in a crash. Because I wanted to be that fast. If the bike wasn't capable of it, I was going to push it till it went into the wall. I realised it wasn't all about how fast I thought I could go. It was how fast the whole package could go.

The culture at Ducati was very cool, very Italian, very stylish, and I really enjoyed that. The Italians nicknamed me Giacomino because James in Italian is 'Giacomo' and one of the big stars out there was Giacomo Agostini. The boss of the championship nicknamed me Giacomino from *'bambino'* meaning baby. It stuck. I used to have it on my leathers. I've got amazing amounts of pull in Italy, because I worked for Ducati for five years and I won the championship for them. I learned quite a lot of Italian, so I'd do my interviews in Italian. And if you'd have seen the Italian brolly girls, it was worth learning Italian for!

On race day, on Sunday morning, the warm-ups were always 9.20 a.m. So at 9.00 a.m. I was in the garage, making sure everything was fine: if we changed anything, what the changes were for the warm-up… and then only 15 minutes to warm up. Do that, come in. Sometimes it was a bit of a shake-down because we only had old tyres to run; it was basically to get warmed up. So we'd run it at about 90 per cent. To speed the brain up as well.

That's a big thing about motorcycle racing. It's amazing how you have to speed up your reactions and perceptions. When you have a couple of months off in the winter – even as a professional – you go down the straight and your brain can't process quickly enough what's happening. After three laps, it was like, OK.

The first bike race was at 10.30 a.m. so one thing I always used to do was go out and see how fast the guy was changing the starting lights that day, because it was always slightly different. I'd watch the first race and count the lights. It was always about two or three seconds: 'On, one, two, three, off.' Just to make sure that we didn't have a quick firer. Was it Linford Christie that said, 'I always try and go on the "b" of the bang'? It's the same concept.

At the start, I used to stand at the side of the bike and bounce like a boxer from foot to foot because, by doing that, it kept my brain up to speed with the concentration level. If I sat doing nothing, it felt like my reactions and concentration were coming down. So I used to just keep moving, keep concentrating. For 45 minutes you could not put a foot wrong. The margin for error is so small. The consequences... it was all about the race. Once you've qualified in a good position, there are two things to do: one was get a good start and keep out of trouble on the first lap, and the second was just concentration. Because in a race, you don't need to ride like in qualifying to get a good position. You just need to hit the same points and times. Consistency. Consistency.

Say you did a 1.50 timed lap to qualify in front. If, in the race, you do 1.51s for 24 laps, you're on the podium. But if you do 1.51, 1.53, 1.52, 1.52, 1.53 and a 1.51, you're tenth. That was how close it was. It was all about keeping up the concentration.

You can only do that with a good team, good confidence, good riding and stay at the front. Because if you're not on a very good bike, you have no choice: you have to ride it hard, sometimes over its limits... and that's why people on slow bikes, in slow cars, crash a lot; because they push beyond the limit. When I was world champion, there were quite a few races where I was in second and third going, 'I'll stay here for a bit.' There were a few where I had to bike hard, but generally the races that I won were the easiest, most comfortable ones.

Even driving on normal roads, my speed perception is good. Really, really simple things that I think everybody knows. Like when I'm on a motorway and I'm doing 70 miles per hour, I know a truck is going at 56 miles per hour and I know how fast I'm going to catch it. It's scarily surprising how many people don't know the speed differences... how quickly you're going to close the gap. On track days as well, I follow people on their bike and it's amazing where they think the limit is. They may be on the brakes fully and I'm still changing gears, still going up. This is why motorsport is so psychological because it's really dangerous. There is, at some point, your own safety level that's going to protect you…

You've got to race it on the limit and to find that limit, so you are going to crash because you have to go over the limit to find it. You can't avoid it.

The trick is never to go over it in a race. Just hover around it.

When I was at my peak, the only thing I was just scared of losing. I wasn't scared of anything else. I had no consideration for safety or thinking it was dangerous, because you would never, ever do the job at that level if you had any feeling for the risk in it. You've got to be in total control and have the confidence to think, 'No matter what I do, everything's going to be fine.'

The worst days were halfway through a race, in fifth or sixth, knowing that the bike's not really working for you or you're not riding it great or you've made a few mistakes and there's nothing you can do to finish where you want to. They were the most frustrating days. And there were quite a few because you can't win 'em all.

The hardest points are the injuries: in hospital for weeks on end recuperating. It's the timescale, because we don't get to sit around in our job. If you can't ride for two races they have to replace you, for the sponsors. They need that bike going round. All we are is moving advertisements so they have to put somebody else on. We know that if we get injured to a certain level, another rider's going to jump on our bike. And you don't want that to happen. Injury is a real inconvenience. You don't think it's a real serious injury for the rest of your life. When I had my leg wrapped around my head, I wasn't thinking, 'Jesus Christ, am I going to be able to walk again?' It was, 'Bloody Hell, I'm going to miss that World Superbike race now.' I was lying on the floor with my leg around my head thinking, 'I've got a race next week!' I could have had my leg amputated. I could have severed my artery. Forty-five minutes lying down there. It could have been serious trouble. Lying there thinking, 'I've got to race next week!' And when I look back at it now, I think I was nuts.

Injuries and hospitals are disappointments. Because when you have a lot of confidence, a lot of belief in yourself and you dedicate your life completely and you achieve the ultimate, it's really, really shocking and disappointing when you don't achieve what you expect. So that's the flip side of it.

And that's a big fall, if you've got that much confidence that you are going to win... if you get knocked on the floor countless times, you've lost. And that's the thing about any professional at the top level. Because you've got to have so much belief in yourself, when it doesn't happen it's very difficult to cope with. And that's the tough part of professional sports.

Real high? Becoming world champion. Crossing the line. Seeing the guy with the chequered flag and looking him in the eye, making sure he's waving it and you haven't missed laps and knowing that forever more you'll have been a world champion.

I was in France at the time and the crowd wasn't that passionate because I beat the French guy – my teammate. It was the last race and I won the world championship over him. It was quite high pressure in France. I was second, he was third. That race won me the world championship. Because you battle all year and it's like: 'I'm in the lead, now I'm second in the championship, now I'm in the lead, now I'm second, now I'm third, Oh s***, I've got to pull it back,' and then the chequered flag – you've got it. A brilliant thing!

What was difficult was two weeks after winning the championship because as a kid, you always wanted that. And when you achieve the ultimate, you need to readjust. All of a sudden it kind of dampened down once I'd achieved the ultimate goal and then I had to find another mentality to keep my head and drive to achieve the same thing again.

So that was another learning curve. The psychological side of sports at the top level – I find it fascinating. Because I've always assessed myself on why I feel the way I do, even in normal life. 'Why do I feel like that? Why am I thinking that?' I've been so lucky to have such emotions. I understand myself a lot more personally, because I've witnessed the really high to the really low. I've been there.

STORY TOLD BY JT

On 23 October 2011 Marco Simoncelli, age 24, was killed in a motorcycle collision with Colin Edwards and Valentino Rossi at the Malaysian Grand Prix. There have been over 200 rider deaths in the Isle of Man TT since 1910.

The Isle of Man TT (Tourist Trophy) Race is one of the most legendary and oldest motorcycle races on the race calendar. The 37-mile mountain course is an extremely challenging track with 200 bends, jumps, stone walls, manhole covers, thousands of spectators and speeds approaching 200 miles per hour. The first race was held in 1907. The winner was Charlie Collier riding a Matchless motorcycle at an average speed of 38 miles per hour. The current lap record is held by John McGuinness on a Honda CBR 1000RR at an average speed of 132 miles per hour.

ACKNOWLEDGEMENTS

My thanks to:

All my fascinating interviewees and contacts who helped me find them.

Those who didn't quite make it into this book – maybe the next one! Gerry the Lighthouse Keeper, Bill the Beefeater, John the Prisoner of War, Chris the Antarctic Engineer, Prakash the Gurkha.

The following charities for their hard work in challenging environments:

**Mission Aviation Fellowship
(www.maf.org)**

**The Royal National Lifeboat Institution
(www.rnli.org.uk)**

**Felix Fund – supporting bomb disposal experts
(www.felixfund.org.uk)**

The following organisations for their hard work in challenging environments:

International Search and Rescue

ACKNOWLEDGEMENTS

The 'Flathead' Hotshot Crew in Montana

HART – Hazardous Area Rescue Teams

Washington State Department of Transportation
(for avalanche clearance)

Silver Lining Tours
(storm chasers)

BIGGEST
FASTEST
DEADLIEST

THE BOOK OF FASCINATING FACTS

DAN BRIDGES

BIGGEST, FASTEST, DEADLIEST

The Book of Fascinating Facts

Dan Bridges

ISBN:978 1 84953 084 2   Hardback   £9.99

THE WORLD'S BIGGEST ISLAND:
Greenland, 840,000 sq miles (2,175,000 km²)

THE WORLD'S FASTEST BIRD:
peregrine falcon, dives after prey at 200 mph (322 km/h)

THE WORLD'S DEADLIEST ANIMAL TO HUMANS:
mosquito, transmits diseases to around 700 million
people annually in Africa, Asia and the Americas

Ever wished you could remember all that stuff you learned at school?
Ever felt the answer to a tie-breaker was on the tip of your tongue?
With this treasure trove of lists you can learn something in your lunch
break and fascinate your mates with facts on astronomy, history,
invention, the natural world and a wealth of other subjects.

Go on, dip in – there's still time to win Mastermind, or at least
a round of Trivial Pursuit!

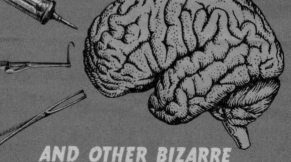

HOW TO REMOVE A BRAIN

AND OTHER BIZARRE MEDICAL PRACTICES AND PROCEDURES

*'Hilarious, and sometimes
stomach-turning, vignettes'*
NEW SCIENTIST

DAVID HAVILAND

HOW TO REMOVE A BRAIN

And Other Bizarre Medical Practices and Procedures

David Haviland

ISBN: 978 1 84953 250 1   Paperback   £7.99

'Hilarious, and sometimes stomach-turning, vignettes'

NEW SCIENTIST

'A must for fans of the bizarre,and perfect prep for livening up dull dinner party conversations.'   **GQ (India)**

Have you ever wondered…

How long it takes to digest chewing gum?

What hiccups are for?

Whether it's safe to fly with breast implants?

Taking in everything from the outrageous (yes, Hitler was addicted to crystal meth) to the eye-watering (such as the renowned surgeon who accidentally cut off his patient's left testicle) to the downright disgusting (like the 'cure' for toothache used by the Egyptians involving dead mouse paste), this book proves that medical science is not for the faint-hearted, lily-livered or weak-stomached!

LOST
IN THE
JUNGLE

A HARROWING
TRUE STORY OF
ADVENTURE
AND
SURVIVAL

YOSSI GHINSBERG

LOST IN THE JUNGLE

A Harrowing Story of Adventure and Survival

Yossi Ghinsberg

ISBN:978 1 84024 672 8   Paperback   £8.99

I heard the rustle again, too close and too real to ignore. I clutched the flashlight, stuck my head out of the mosquito net... and found myself face-to-face with a jaguar.

Four travellers meet in Bolivia and set off into the Amazon rainforest on an expedition to find a hidden tribe and explore places tourists only dream of seeing. But what begins as the adventure of a lifetime quickly becomes a struggle for survival when they get lost in the wilds of the jungle.

The group splits up after disagreements, and Yossi and his friend try to find their own way back without a guide. But when a terrible rafting accident separates them, Yossi is forced to survive for weeks alone in one of the most unpredictable environments on the planet. Stranded without a knife, map or survival training, he must improvise shelter and forage for wild fruit to survive. As his skin begins to rot from his feet during raging storms and he loses all sense of direction, he wonders if he will make it back alive.

It's a story of friendship and of the teachings of the forest, and a terrifying true account that you won't be able to put down.

Have you enjoyed this book?
If so, why not write a review on your favourite website?

If you're interested in finding out more about our books
follow us on Twitter: **@Summersdale**

Thanks very much for buying this Summersdale book.

www.summersdale.com